WHAT THEY SEE

Library and Archives Canada Cataloguing in Publication

Swanson, Jennifer, 1967-, author
    What they see : how to stand out and shine in your new
job / Jennifer Swanson.

Includes bibliographical references.
Issued in print and electronic formats.
ISBN 978-1-77141-099-1 (pbk.).--ISBN 978-1-77141-100-4 (html)

1. Success in business. 2. Career development. 3. Interpersonal
communication. I. Title.

HF5386.S95 2015   650.1   C2015-901228-7
                                            C2015-901229-5

What They See

How to stand out
and shine in your new job

Jennifer Swanson

First Published in Canada 2015 by Influence Publishing

Book Cover Design: Trista Baldwin
Cover Photographer: Amanda Waschuk
Cover Model: Mike Rioden
Editor: Susan Kehoe
Assistant Editor: Nina Shoroplova
Production Editor: Jennifer Kaleta
Typeset: Greg Salisbury
Portrait Photographer: Ryan McNeill Bolton

This book is dedicated with love to

Katie and Ben: for bringing untold joy to my life

Scott: for your love, encouragement, and unfailing support

Emma and Sarah: for your delightful enthusiasm

Bruce: for the hilarity

Mom: for always cheering me on

And to Little Bandit:
for keeping my feet warm while I wrote this book.

Testimonials

In her casual, personal and down-to-earth style, Jenn has provided the reader with an easy to follow guide for a successful start to one's working career. The communication, professional and self-awareness tips offered will help anyone to present themselves well and to become a valuable member of any organization.

Sandy Chernoff, RDH, B.Sc., Owner: Soft Skills for Success, Author: 5 *Secrets to Effective Communication* www.softskillsforsuccess.com

A light-hearted primer for succeeding at your first job. Swanson advises on everything from handling gossip, what to wear, recovering from mistakes, and curbing a bad attitude.

Dr. Jennifer Newman, R.Psych., Founder of Newman Psychological and Consulting Services

Acknowledgements

There are many people who inspired, influenced, and motivated me to write this book. I would like to firstly thank my many students over the years who have asked really good questions, shared stories, and always asked for more. I delight in seeing your success.

I have many regular readers and podcast listeners at CommunicationDiva.com to thank for being interested in better relationships through effective communication. For the thousands of you who tune in or come to the website each month, I sincerely thank you.

To the gurus whose books I read, whose podcasts I listen to, and whom I follow online: you have taught me so much: Fr. Richard Rohr, Daniel B. Goleman, Seth Godin, and Pat Flynn.

To Cliff Ravenscraft and the Podcast Mastermind Alumni: my friends your support, encouragement, technical help, and guidance has been invaluable.

To the people of Northwood United, Crossroads United, and Ioco United Churches: you are always in my heart.

To the Java Lovers Women in Business Group: thank you for the friendship and the opportunities to learn and connect with motivated and energetic entrepreneurs.

To Sandy Chernoff for your mentorship. You are the reason I actually began this book-writing adventure, and I hope I'm like you when I finally grow up!

To Lynn Oucharek, Shelley-Anne Vidal, Sydney Silva, Georgina Handley, and Valerie Thompson for your collaboration, support, and contributions.

To my teaching colleagues, and my ministry colleagues,

who listened, shared ideas, and showed enthusiasm for this project: thank you.

To Julie Salisbury and the staff of Influence Publishing for making my dream a reality.

To Sue Kehoe and Nina Shoroplova for your honesty, guidance, and hard work with editing and proofreading the manuscript.

And finally, to my beautiful family and my dear friends who are too numerous to name:

I am so very blessed to have each one of you in my life.

Jenn Swanson

Contents

Before We Get Into It (An Introduction)

Congratulations! If you are reading this, I am guessing that you:

a. just graduated and are ready to enter the workforce,
b. have just been hired for a new job and want some fast and concrete advice,
c. are being asked to read it by a teacher, parent, or career counsellor,
d. found it at a garage sale and thought it looked interesting.
(Never mind that last one.)

Whatever the case, I am congratulating you because you obviously care about how you present yourself to your new employer and I want to help you do that well; so well, in fact, that you stand out from the crowd and shine.

I want you to blind and bedazzle them with your brilliant professionalism!

I want you to succeed and to know that it is entirely possible.

So How Can I Help?

I wear a number of hats and one of the things I do is teach in the healthcare field in a community college. Most of my students are training to go into a workplace setting they have never been in before. Part of what I teach them is how to succeed when they are out in their clinical placements and ultimately when they are out in the workforce once graduated. I use a number of stories and examples in this book from my work in supervising students on the job to explain some of the topics. I also have spent a fair bit of time with youth while wearing another hat of mine: that of a church minister and, from 2010 to 2013, I worked specifically as a youth minister. I learn a lot from the people I work with.

Another hat, and one of the best ones ever to learn from, is being a mom and a stepmom to four teenage and young adult children. We've talked a lot about the topic of workplace communication and something my son said has always stuck with me: "My generation thinks we're so good at communicating because we do it all the time with texting and stuff, but really, we are some of the worst communicators I know." He said that when he was about eighteen, and he was talking about his own circle of friends and acquaintances, but it made me wonder if there were some way that I, wearing all my hats and with the education and work experience I have, could help.

Another hat I wear, and one that is a lot of fun because it is so creative, is being a podcaster, blogger, and workshop leader. I believe that effective communication leads to deeper and more harmonious relationships, both in home life and in the workplace, and I am passionate about inspiring and encouraging people to grow and to succeed.

Since the launch of my website in 2011 and my podcast in 2012 (both found at www.communicationdiva.com), I have noticed that the majority of the daily search-engine searches have involved questions about how to "be" at work, how to be professional, what to wear, how to impress the boss, how to get ahead, etc.

An article I wrote in October 2011 about what to wear to work is *still* getting daily views, and that tells me that people are looking for this kind of help. The article gives a clear description of what would be considered professional to wear in most office or workplace settings, and what would be inappropriate. Because the article has had such a long lifespan in the world of blog posts, I got curious about what other workplace-related topics people were searching for. I wrote more articles and did more podcasts, and eventually I wondered how I could compile these into something that people would find helpful.

I wanted there to be a non-textbook version of how to succeed at work (how to be professional, how to show up as an above-average employee, how to be sure you *stay* employed past the probationary period). Because I teach this stuff to college students and offer workshops on my website, and because much of what I want to share doesn't seem to be available in one consolidated book format, and, being the kind, caring, helpful person that I am (cue the sappy music here), I decided that maybe I could assist and write one myself.

I know that it's hard out there. I work with students who are finishing high school and college, and looking for work in a competitive job market. How they present themselves before, during, and *after* the interview is key. My students always have many questions about how to present themselves in ways that will help them to succeed. I never seem to have enough time in the classroom schedule to answer their concerns, and that's because there is a lot to think about when getting ready to start a new job. There are a lot of books, articles, and websites out there about interviewing, so I'm not going to spend time discussing that; instead, I want to help you **show up on Day One** of your job and help you prove to the person who hired you that they made the right decision.

In fact, I'd love to think that that person was congratulated for making such a good choice by hiring you.

I want you to be able to walk into the workplace on your first day, to look professional and act professionally, and to be ready to take on whatever is thrown your way.

I also took the liberty to assume a few things about you, the reader.

I assume:

- you want to be the best "You" possible in this new job and that includes being seen as professional no matter what role you are in;
- you are looking for quick, simple, actionable steps that you can put into place immediately; and
- you just finished school, are ready to start your first job and get busy putting all that learning into action (not to mention putting some much needed cash in your pocket).

In this book, I provide you with advice, tips, strategies, and tried-and-true methods so you can present yourself as a true professional the very first day you step into your new workplace. The information here applies to all sorts of workplace settings, and to those of you working virtually from home as well. If you interact with others in *any* format during your work day, there is something here for you.

I will teach you what a professional is and how to "be" a professional on Day One of your new job and throughout the first few months of the typical probation period. I want your new employer to say they made an **excellent choice in you as a new employee** right from the very beginning.

Are you ready? Let's go!

Chapter One

You Got the Job—Now What?

There's more to success in the workplace than a fabulous resume.

Okay, so you mastered the interview. Congratulations! You dazzled them with your brilliance. Now what? What happens now that you have the job?

In this chapter, I will tell you about the qualities employers are looking for in a new employee and I will teach you how to be the best and most professional employee you can be—particularly in the crucial first few months (the dreaded "probationary period").

Making That First Impression

We have all heard the expression "you only have seven seconds to make a good first impression." However, a series of experiments by Princeton psychologists Janine Willis and Alexander Todorov[1] dismisses the idea that you have seven seconds to impress, and suggests that you actually only have one tenth of a second for someone to judge you favourably. From the moment you extend your hand to say hello, opinions have been formed. This does not mean

---

[1]Todorov, Alexander and Janine Willis. "First Impressions: Making Up Your Mind After a 100-Ms Exposure to a Face."Psychological Science, Vol 17:7. Princeton University, July 2006. psych.princeton.edu/psychology/research/todorov/pdf/Willis&Todorov-PsychScience.pdf accessed January 30, 2015

opinions cannot be changed, modified, or reversed over time, but it does literally make that first moment key.

And then what?

What's next?

What's next is that first few months after that first impression ... that time of orientation and starting to learn the ropes and what is often a time of employment probation. This trial period is equally as important as the first impression made and is, in fact, critical to you keeping your new job and succeeding in the months to come.

You want it to work out.

How you present yourself (everything from what you wear, to what you say and do), will set the foundation for how successful you are in the job in the long run.

As a new employee there are many things outside your control, that you can't do much about ... and there are also quite a few things that are in your full control and that you can do a lot about. So it is important to be aware of these things and know how you can manage them.

What this **isn't** about is making you into a robot lacking in creativity, initiative, critical thinking, and innovative ideas; a robot who simply does the work and gets paid. Anyone can do that, and that kind of employee is not going to stand out or shine or change the world. That kind of employee is not particularly special or interesting or critical to how well the company functions.

That kind of employee is expendable. You are not that kind of robot.

What this **is** about is having some "cool tools" in your toolkit. What it's about is being aware of how you come across to others, and how you can monitor and change that if you need to. What it is about is becoming a valuable (shall

I dare to say "indispensable"?) part of your work team.

What it's about is **you**, and being the best "you" you can be.

And so, I'm going to walk you through some of the things that will make a difference beyond the first millisecond. Some of these things you might already know and feel like you've already mastered, and if that's the case, consider this a refresher.

Some of them will be new for you.

Whatever the case, I've been the new employee several times myself, and have coached dozens of people who are starting new jobs, many of them in workplace environments they have never experienced before, so I have a few tips and ideas for you, and a few stories to share along the way.

One of the first things you might feel—after the excitement of actually being told you have the job—is nervous. It's hard being new to the team.

Part of what makes you as a new employee nervous is that you'll be in orientation and likely on probation or have a trial period at the start of your job. Thinking of this period as an *opportunity* is a good place to begin. Instead of it being a time of testing (to see if you're actually any good and whether or not they'll keep you), think of it as a chance to shine. This is a learning time when you are expected to ask a lot of questions. Take charge of your own learning, and be proactive in it. People are usually very willing to help you, and as long as you are not abusing their generosity, as long as you are working hard, people are willing to help you succeed.

This learning time (orientation, probation, trial period) is not a time to sit around waiting for people to tell you what you are supposed to be doing, but rather a time to set yourself some daily learning goals, and to evaluate each of them at the end of the day. This is a time to get curious, and to ask questions and keep notes that you can look over and review later. Find out how things are done, who does them, and what your responsibility is in the mix. This time of getting to know your new workplace and the people in it can be very rich.

It's also exhausting, because there is so much to learn.

Being nervous about starting your new job (and being tired at the start) is entirely normal. So is making mistakes, and we'll talk more about that later.

So, What Does it Mean to "Be" Professional?

Let's talk about something you **know** is important and I'm sure you've been told you need to be at work: professional.

"Be professional," *they* tell you. "Act like a professional." "He's very professional at work." "She looks very professional," and so on. You've heard it. I've heard it. It seems like something to aspire to. Of course, you should be professional at work.

But what does that actually mean?

And how can you *be* it if you aren't clear about what *it* is?

You have prepared really well for the interview and have blown them away. They've decided to take a chance on you ... to hire you. You are new and you want to make a good impression.

Better yet, you want to make an EXCELLENT impression ... without looking like you are too eager or inauthentic.

You got this job ... and now (quite simply), you want to

keep it and do well in it.

Being professional is what we are focusing on here.

Being professional, rather than being "a" professional, speaks more to *how* you do things, how you behave, how you respond, etc., rather than what qualifications you have.

I consider a professional to be a person with good manners, one who has respect, who cares and is concerned for others as well as for him or herself, and who exhibits businesslike conduct in the workplace. A professional does the job well and takes pride in the work done.

With this definition, *EVERYONE* can behave in a professional manner, and those who do, **get noticed**.

In a good way.

How you do your job, how you carry yourself and present yourself to others, how you manage your time, how you speak (both in terms of the words and the tone of voice you use), what you wear, and what values you hold dear ALL contribute to a sense of professionalism ... and the secret is ... (drum roll here) ... **You CAN be professional no matter what it is you are doing!**

How to Style a Sandwich Professionally

There is a woman who works in the cafeteria at a local training institute. This cafeteria is a busy place at lunchtime, and one of the stations is the sandwich-making station where this woman works.

I watched her in fascination one day while I was there doing some coach training. She was incredibly professional. She looked each person in the eye and smiled as they came up to her station. She offered them bread choice, spreads, fillings, and took great care as she spread the spreads, placed the filling in the sandwich, cut it nicely, and plated it. She was not just making a sandwich; she was styling it! She was putting her best effort into making the best sandwich she could craft, and the interesting thing was ... people would wait. It probably took her longer than it needed to, but because of her professional and obviously caring attitude, people appreciated her work.

What made it *professional* was that she cared about the needs of the person she was serving, she did her work very well, and she was proud of it. And she stood out because of that. I happily waited in the line-up on several occasions just to watch her work. And of course, the results were delicious.

What if everyone applied these principles to the work they do, no matter what kind of job it is?

Pay attention to *how* people approach work and see if you can spot those who act professionally and those who do not.

Seth Godin said in his audiobook *Linchpin*, "You are not your resume. You are your work."[2] I think what he means by that is you are not what you list on a sheet of paper, all the accomplishments and itemizations of what you have learned and can do (all important, of course), but you are what you *do* and *how* you do it. You can say you possess all sorts of skills and diplomas and certificates, but until

---

[2]Godin, Seth. *Linchpin: Are You Indispensable?* New York: Portfolio/Penguin, 2010, audioversion

you show people in real time what it is you are capable of, the resume is just a piece of paper. You have the ability to *show* people what you're made of, which is far more than just following the rules and being mediocre. You have the chance to shine ... to be the best you can be at whatever it is you are doing ... to connect with others and become more than just another employee, but one who is a key player in the organization.

You want to become necessary.

ELEVEN ATTRIBUTES OF A TRUE PROFESSIONAL

A true professional possesses all or most of these essential attributes:

- [ ] a positive attitude
- [ ] a handle on WHY they are there in the first place
- [ ] expertise in their area
- [ ] a good work ethic
- [ ] accountability
- [ ] awareness of their limitations
- [ ] fantastic communication skills
- [ ] humility
- [ ] gratitude
- [ ] generosity
- [ ] a willingness to learn

Do you possess all or most of these essential attributes? What, if anything, could you work on to instantly improve your professionalism? We will be exploring these attributes in detail in this book, and I will offer you ways in which to improve in the areas you choose to work on.

Are You an Expert?

Professionals are experts in their fields.

Of course, at the beginning, you might not be. You have all the training and theory you need to get started, but you may not yet have the experience to be able to call yourself an "expert." Professional athletes become so because they spend years practising. Professional artists spend years learning their craft. Professional lawyers spend years studying and practising. Professional thereminists—theremin players—well, you get the picture.3

You are, however, well on your way to being professional. Your willingness to learn in your new position is key to moving you forward. Take notes. Ask questions. Be constantly curious about how things work and why things are done a certain way in your workplace. If there are policy and procedure manuals, read them. If there are training videos, watch them. If you need to know more, get training, read books and blogs, find someone to mentor you, and learn as much as you can.

While your expertise in the work itself is very important, it is only one part of the whole in the quest for professional behaviour. Most people with a little instruction can costruct a sandwich, for example. Professionalism is less about what it is you do, and more about how you do it, what you know about it, how you share that knowledge, and how you interact with others as you work.

3The theremin is one of the strangest instruments I've ever heard of. You don't actually touch it to play it! It began as a scientific sensory instrument invented by Russian physicist Leon Theremin (his Westernized name) in 1920 and later patented in 1928. Look it up on the internet and you'll find videos where you can hear its eerie and haunting sound.

It takes time, effort, and desire to be an expert at whatever it is you choose to do, and no, you won't actually be one at the beginning ... but you CAN be an "expert-in-training" the moment you begin your job.

Nine Skills Your Employer Wants You to Have

This next list is something you can keep coming back to. Check and see if you can honestly say you have all these skills, and if you need to work on a few, then choose one at a time, set each as a goal, and work on reaching each goal over a period of time.

Organizational Skills

Are you good at keeping things straight, prioritizing, and knowing where to find the things you need at a moment's notice? Is your workspace neat? Can you get through your to-do list? Can you develop a plan of action when given multiple tasks to complete in a day? Can you anticipate what needs to happen and set the wheels in motion to make it a reality? Being able to organize and execute a plan are important skills that employers value.

Self-Motivation/Initiative

Do you work on tasks assigned to you on your own, or do you wait for someone to tell you what to do next? If you see something that needs to be done, do you do it? Employers want to see you busy, engaged, and thinking on behalf of the team. If you can be self-motivated and take initiative, you'll be shining soon enough. You'll also enjoy the benefit of a little more creative freedom and autonomy if you can work it out so that you don't have to be told exactly what to do and how to do it every single time.

CONFIDENCE

Of course at first you might not feel superconfident as an employee, because you will be asking a lot of questions and learning the ropes, but even in your uncertainty, you can be confident. You can let people know where you need help and where you feel capable, and work from there. Confidence in your role will build as you gain experience. People will respect you if you tell them you'd like some feedback around your performance, or that you'd like reminders if they see you forgetting something you need to be doing. Stating that you recognize you are learning and wanting some guidance from the people who know what they are doing will help you to feel more confident and help your co-workers feel more confident in you.

COMMUNICATION SKILLS

Many people state they have "excellent" communication skills on their resumes these days as a matter of course, and I am not sure what that means anymore. Does this mean you are fabulous at written communication? Verbal communication? Can you write well, or are you a social media whiz? Developing good communications skills requirespractice, and is, in fact, a practice, rather than something you can master and be done with. Communication is always evolving, and there is always more to learn. As long as you are willing to continually work on your communication skills, to actively improve and grow your skills, then you will be an asset to your employer.

INDUSTRY AWARENESS

You are new on the job, yes, but that doesn't mean you haven't done your research ... right? You learned as much as you could about your industry before you got the job, and you are continuing to learn as you go, reading articles and blogs about it, watching videos if they exist, reading industry-related publications, etc. Understanding your industry or the company you work for will help keep you on the "cutting edge" and allow you to have relevant con-versations with co-workers and management. You will be viewed as interested, engaged, and knowledgeable, which of course will make you stand out.

A "TEAM PLAYER" ATTITUDE

In most workplaces, you will be working with one or more people, and sometimes a group or a team of people. The ability to work well in a group, as a team player, is a sought-after quality that many employers look for in new employees. Working well in a group or a team environment is an active process, one that is going to test out your previously mentioned excellent communication skills!

STRESS MANAGEMENT SKILLS

Can you work under pressure? How well do you handle stressful situations? What kinds of tools and supports do you need in place to be able to stand up to the demands of the job? These are things it would be really useful to know about yourself, and to be able to work on if you find you crumble or fall apart when things get hard. Your boss wants to trust that you can handle what comes at you, and so working on how to do that in times of non-stress is a good way to get started.

- Know your stress triggers.
- Know your own body and the signals it sends when you are under pressure.
- Know what helps you to relieve stress.
- Figure out how to prevent stress from happening in the first place, by being organized, meeting deadlines, and taking the initiative. Anticipate problems, and then work out how to prevent them.

LEADERSHIP SKILLS

You might not have them yet, but you can work your way up to being a leader by taking on small projects, by taking the initiative and making decisions on your own (within the scope of your role, of course), and by being willing to step outside of what feels safe and to risk a little. There are a lot of amazing books in bookstores and online, and courses on leadership available through colleges, universities, and other sources. If you are at all interested in "climbing the corporate ladder" as they say, then you might seriously give some time to developing skills in this area. Ask your new employer if they offer leadership training.

PROBLEM-SOLVING SKILLS

These go along with taking the initiative and being a leader. What happens when something goes wrong and you need to figure out how to fix it? We'll be talking more about this in Chapter 8, but for now, you can improve these skills by not running to a supervisor or co-worker every single time you run across a problem, but instead, by thinking about how you can solve it on your own first. Now if someone is in serious danger, or if the problem is too big for you to handle on your own (or as a new employee) then, of course, ask for help ... but there are going to be small things that come up that you can quite easily resolve on your own, and doing that will build up both your confidence and your ability with this skill set.

WHAT'S IN IT FOR YOU?

In other words, what do you **get** out of being professional in your work?

You get:

- support
- respect
- trust
- recognition
- opportunity

SUPPORT

Both management and your co-workers will offer you support in busy and challenging times if they see you as having a professional attitude. At the start of a new job, you're the "newbie," and everyone knows that you have a lot to learn about your role and how the place functions. If people get the sense that you are approaching your work with care, that you are proud of what you do, and that doing well is important to you, you'll get the help, support, and guidance from those around you.

Even once you are fully trained and past your probationary period, support is important. In fact, it's critical if you ever want to advance in your job, if you want to try implementing your new and creative ideas, or if issues arise or crises happen and you need to lean on those around you in order to manage. It's a much more productive and fun environment to be in if you feel like people "have your back" and vice-versa.

Respect

We'll talk more about boundary-setting and how to get even more respect in a later chapter, but having a professional attitude is going to get you respect from your boss, the management, your co-workers, your customers or clients, and most importantly ... from yourself! You will respect yourself more if you know deep down inside that you are behaving in a way that others can admire. It's hard to work in a job without respect. In fact, it's pretty miserable. Lack of respect can involve gossip behind your back, negative feedback, and can be the ruin of a team.

So respect is a real win in your favour.

Trust

Trust is one of the major benefits of being professional at

work. Earning the trust of your co-workers makes for a friendlier and more fun atmosphere. Earning the trust of your manager, supervisor, or boss could mean you get to try new and more interesting things as you gain confidence in your position and are able to handle work that is more challenging. The trust of your clients or customers, or whoever benefits from the work that you do, is invaluable. You can't buy that trust, and you can't force it to happen.

You have to earn it.

Much of my working career at the beginning was in the healthcare world. People who come into hospital because they are sick are often in an unfamiliar place and are scared. In many cases, if a person, even someone not directly related to the medical care of the patient, does their job in a professional way, it will help to make the patient feel a bit less scared.

"Okay, these people obviously know what's going on. I can feel confident that I'll be looked after here."

If you can gain the trust of the people you are serving, you will also gain their respect and their confidence in you and your work. Gaining trust is worth a lot more than you might think.

And trust lost is hard to get back.

You want people to trust you, and acting professionally will help that happen.

RECOGNITION

You may not get formal recognition (awards, employee of the month, company cars)—although that would be fabulous—but being professional will get you the kind of recognition that is actually worth more than all of that.

People will seek your opinion. They will see you as **competent**, **responsible**, and above all, **an asset** to the company or organization.

You will be recognized as valuable and that will get you places.

And you never know ... maybe it'll get you a big fat Christmas bonus.

OPPORTUNITY

Being seen to be professional for the work you do, even if you are still new and learning how it all works, will earn you future opportunities that may not be given to others who are less professional in manner.

If you are showing up, doing your work, interested, engaged, and willing to learn, your boss or manager is going to notice. If you demonstrate leadership qualities, no matter what job you have, you will be noticed. It increases the chance that your name will come up if something new needs to be done, and it puts you in a better position for advancement and future opportunities.

So support, respect, trust, recognition, and opportunity are at least five of the benefits of showing your professional side. With all of that good stuff, why wouldn't you want to?

Much of professionalism begins with attitude.

Chapter Two

Attitude

Attitude Is Everything!

There are many benefits to having a positive attitude: benefits for you and for those you work with. Attitude is contagious, and people are drawn more easily and readily to those who are positive and happy on a consistent basis.

People with positive attitudes appear more confident, more competent, and more successful. People who are optimistic, hopeful, and constructive tend toward creative thinking, have higher energy, and feel more motivated.

It's fun and energizing to be around someone who has positive energy!

I am not suggesting that you need to be false in your attitude if you are not someone who has a consistently positive attitude, but rather that you take the time to notice what attitude you naturally default to, and then decide whether or not you want to improve on it. Even if you do naturally default to the positive side, there will be opportunity for you to grow and develop your skills, particularly if you are working with a co-worker who doesn't share your sunny disposition.

A bad attitude can be bad for business. Here are two common experiences we have all encountered.

You walk into a store and the person behind the customer service desk treats you with hostility or disdain, as if you are interrupting them for no apparent reason, instead of being the valuable client or customer that you are. How does that make you feel?

You walk into a store where the salesperson greets you immediately, asks how your day is going, and seems genuinely interested in helping you. Now, how does that make you feel?

Based on how you are treated and how it makes you feel, which store would you shop at again?

Attitude is a very potent and important part of the communication mix, and has everything to do with how professionally you come across to others.

Be aware of the attitude you are projecting and make sure it is positive when you walk in the office door, even if you've had a horrible start to your day.

"How can I do that?" you might ask. "What if I really have had a horrible day?"

Then be honest.

It's perfectly okay to tell your boss, manager, or your co-workers that you aren't feeling great and that you've had a rough start to the day. You don't need to go into detail. Your co-workers will understand as they have had bad days too. You might be quieter than usual that day, but make sure you aren't snapping or snarling at other people. They are, after all, innocent bystanders.

Blessing the rest of the world with your misery is inappropriate and a very quick way to be unprofessional. If you are having a really bad day or find you often have a negative attitude at work, there are things you can do.

Some might suggest you fake it, that you pretend you are in a good mood until eventually you are. This might not work all the time or for the long term, but it can at least take the edge off and give others around you a break.

Of course, if something really serious is going on, the best course of action is to ask someone for help.

For most of us, the key to changing a negative attitude into a positive one is figuring out what is causing our "bad" attitude—why we are having such a hard time of it.

HERE ARE A FEW QUESTIONS YOU MIGHT ASK YOURSELF:

1. Does your less-than-positive attitude have anything to do with your job?
2. Do you really like this job? Is it worth it?
3. Is there something realistic you can do about who or what's bothering you ... and if yes, what would be the first step?
4. Once you notice your poor attitude, can you make a conscious choice to take a break from the negativity and focus on the task at hand? (Not always possible, but it's a good question to ask yourself.)
5. Is the story you are telling yourself about being in a bad mood and having a bad day or year or life really true? Or is it your brain making things more dramatic than they actually are, which the brain so often tends to do?
6. What *good* things have happened to you today that you can focus on instead? Make a list and look at it. (You woke up this morning, for one thing. The cute barista smiled at you as she made your morning latte. You made it to work on time with no accidents. You have a paying job to go to.) There are likely many things to be grateful for ... and it can be really helpful to list them, count them, and pay attention to them.

7. Ask yourself what you are gaining by having a bad attitude, and ask yourself what you might be losing because of it.

The *most* professional people are those who do their jobs with a positive, pleasant attitude almost *all the time.* Of course, it's impossible to actually be positive and pleasant one hundred percent of the time (and there are times when that might even be inappropriate), but aiming to present yourself that way as often as you can will get noticed in a good way.

HUMILITY, GRATITUDE, AND GENEROSITY

OH LORD, IT'S HARD TO BE HUMBLE!

Humility means being humble. It means you are modest in your opinion of yourself, and that you give credit where credit is due. Humility means that no matter who you are, how important or rich or famous or talented you are, you are not better than other people, nor are you always right. If you are humble, you think of others, and are able to put the needs of others before your own.

I recently interviewed a Canadian celebrity who is on a national television program; he is the man behind four acclaimed British Columbia-based restaurants (soon to be five!), an award-winning food truck, his own name brand frozen food line, two published cookbooks, and is known as one of the best Indian chefs in the world. Vikram Vij said in our conversation that the reason he refuses to take reservations at any of his restaurants, no matter who wants to book a table, is because we all have to eat, and in that regard as well as in many others, we are all the same. He also says that taking reservations is costly to a business, and in order to keep the food prices affordable for people, everyone is considered to be a VIP, and everyone has to wait. Even the Prime Minister of Canada, Pierre Trudeau, had to wait for a table like everyone else who lined up for hours to get in! Food is the great equalizer, and my biggest impression of this famous, successful, and accomplished man is that he possesses humility, and I respect him for that.

Humility is a large part of being seen as a professional and as a great employee. No one likes a person who toots their own horn (an old expression, but cute nonetheless), or who brags incessantly about how brilliant they are. Do you know people like that?

It's NOT okay.

A professional doesn't need to tell anyone that they are a professional. It will be self-evident.

It's all about how you conduct yourself—how you actually behave—that speaks the loudest.

Humility will take you far.

This doesn't mean you can't be proud of your accomplishments, or that you can't let people know about what you are doing and what you know; not at all. It's good to be able to say (out loud ... to others) that you know how to do something or that you have some knowledge in the area, or that you have ideas that might work.

Raving on about how amazing you are, however, is a big turn-off, and is just simply not smart.

People will start avoiding you.

If you turn every conversation into one about you, people will stop talking to you.

Be curious about others. Ask about them and listen hard to what they say so you can remember it and ask them about it later.

"How was the concert you went to on the weekend? You were excited about it when you told me about it. Was it awesome?"

People who are interested in other people are the most interesting themselves.

Being humble means many things, such as these:

- being interested in those around you (not self-absorbed)
- acknowledging others who had a role in something you've done that is receiving praise
- sharing the glory and giving credit where credit is due
- accepting compliments and kudos graciously
- saying thank-you, often

This might be an area you need to work on ... and that's okay. It's better to be completely honest with yourself about what areas need work. Get out a highlighter and highlight parts of this book (as long as you own it!) that you want to work on, and then get busy.

We all have areas we could work on, and we have nothing to lose and a lot to gain by taking some time to invest in ourselves in this way. Self-growth is one of those terms that I realize has baggage attached to it; however, it really just means paying attention to your own stuff and getting to know yourself better.

PRACTISE GRATITUDE

In my humble opinion, there is not enough gratitude going on in the workplace ... or anywhere for that matter.

If someone does something nice for you, thank them.

If you notice someone doing an excellent job, compliment them on it.

If someone does you a favour, be grateful. Send a little note (via real mail if you want to really impress, or virtual, which is faster and easier but not as chic) to thank people for things they have helped you with or done for you.

Say thank-you to the bus driver, the person who delivers the mail or the newspaper, the person who makes your morning coffee, or the person who stocks the grocery shelves and helps you find something.

Words are extremely powerful, and sometimes using them to express that for which you are grateful will make more of a difference in the world than you can imagine.

I worked for three years in a busy Emergency Department. It was understaffed, had very little space, was the only hospital in a growing seaside community that was near the Canada/US border, and it had a railway line running through it. There was a large retired population in the town, and more and more families were moving in. We treated everything from heart attacks to near-drownings, train accidents to drug smugglers coming in with the border guards to "relieve" themselves of evidence.

It was a zoo, and extremely busy.

One night ... late ... after a really hard and emotionally heavy shift (several deaths and hard-to-see situations, huge waiting room numbers, and really sick people) the ER doctor in charge called us all together in the Nursing

Station. He looked each of us in the eye, and said something like this:

"Tonight was insane. We all worked really hard. I want each of you to know that I appreciate working with you. We make a great team. I want you to know that together we did good work tonight, and we made a difference. Thank you."

Out of all the shifts I did in my twenty-three years of working in the hospital system, that one moment stands out among the best. Why? Because it was heartfelt, spontaneous, welcomed, and real. He gave us a gift of gratitude, and we went home at nearly midnight feeling satisfied that we'd done our best in a tough situation, and that as hard as it was physically and emotionally, we had made a difference.

Say thank-you often, and mean it.

It's important and I believe it can change your life.

How to Practise Gratitude

It's a skill, like any other, and practising being grateful is a muscle that can be built up with repetition. If negativity is your default, then every time you notice yourself complaining or about to complain, balance it out with making a list (even mentally) of something you are glad and grateful about.

Keep a list somewhere visible of the things in your life that you are thankful for. Journal at the end of each day, even if it's a bulleted list of three to five things that happened that day that you are grateful for.

If there are people on the list, let them know about it.

Be Generous

Professionals are generous with what they know. Hoarding information for personal gain is not the sign of a real professional. Sharing information and being generous with it will prove you are confident in who you are and what you do, and will always serve you better in the end.

Generosity doesn't only mean money.

If you stay after work to help someone with a computer problem, you are being generous with your time. If you go out of your way to offer someone a compliment on something they did, you are being generous. If you know how to do something and offer to show another person what you know, you are being generous. If you know they are allergic to gluten (like me), and bake them gluten-free chocolate fudge brownies, you are amazing!

An Ability and a Willingness to Learn

I once asked a man in an interview setting how much continuing education time he thought he might need. He very arrogantly crossed his legs and said, "I've got my doctorate. I'm done with learning."

Needless to say, I wasn't impressed.

I don't think we are ever "done with learning." Ever.

There is always something new that will come along that could make your job better, more interesting, easier, or more cutting edge. There are always courses, training sessions, seminars, books, or webinars to take in. Technology is constantly changing, techniques and policies get updated, curricula change, and so does terminology. The willingness to learn new things will keep you current and up to industry standard, and even beyond, no matter what your industry is.

If you want to think you are "done," you will eventually get left in the dust.

Next, we'll take a look at your outside package: what messages are you sending that you might not be aware of? What are other people seeing? How can you pay more attention to how you show up, and what can you do to make a difference?

There are some very simple, practical things that you can do immediately to improve your professional image. Let's dive in and get you shining.

Chapter Three

What am I Supposed to Wear? Dress Code and More

Every single day without fail, someone finds my website by searching "what to wear in a professional setting."

Every single day.

Apparently, it's a question a lot of people are asking, and so I thought I would spend a little time exploring what clothing communicates, and what to wear to work.

What Does Your Clothing Say About You?

It actually says quite a lot. Whether the message you send with your clothing accurately represents you or not is moot, because the person receiving the message forms an opinion of you in an instant and what people perceive, they believe. It is this moment of communication that you can control, if you are conscious of it.

A study done in 2013 in the UK and Turkey looked at the influence of the clothing a person wears on first impressions. Four images were shown to the 274 participants for a maximum of five seconds each. The four images were of two male models with their faces obscured, showing only their clothing, ensuring that the snap judgments made were on clothing alone. The models were of the same build and height, and wore the same shoes. Only their suits changed, with each man wearing one off-the-rack suit in one image and a suit tailored to fit in the other. The suits were of the same colour and material. Each participant was then asked to answer a short series of questions about their perceptions of the men in the images based on their quick viewing of them. The results of the study determined that the clothing a person wears can communicate important qualities about them such as sociability, character, competence, affluence, and intelligence, and all in a fraction of a second.[4] The study went on to say that clothing itself is a powerful communication tool, and can influence the assumptions people make about others. Whether or not the person is flexible, trustworthy, successful, and earns a high salary can all be decided by the viewer in an instant.

Another component of the study found that the clothing a person wears affects how they feel about themselves. Interestingly, men believe more strongly than women do that the way they dress has a strong impact in a professional setting. Men believe they are communicating more clearly that they are competent, knowledgeable, intelligent, honest, and reliable when dressed appropriately. Women believe this too, only not as strongly as men do, according to this study.

The snap judgements others make about us in less than a second are worth paying attention to. While we have no control over what people do with the perceptions they have, we can put some time and attention into conveying the messages we intend to by not overlooking this key form of communication.

---

[4]N. Howlett, K. Pine, I. Orakcioglu, and B. Fletcher. "The influence of clothing on first impressions: Rapid and positive responses to minor changes in male attire." *Journal of Fashion Marketing and Management*, 17(1), 38-48, 2013.

Flight attendants and pilots usually look extremely well-groomed, tidy, and professional. The reason for this runs more deeply than company dress code protocol. A person who looks well put together conveys confidence, efficiency, and (more importantly when in mid-air) competence. In the unlikely event of an airline emergency, passengers want to know there are competent and capable people in charge.

I have walked into office settings where people are dressed in business suits and conservative dresses, and the receptionist is in jeans and an off-the-shoulder sweatshirt (think *Flashdance*). I wondered how she got the job in the first place, whether she was a regular employee or someone's daughter filling in in a pinch, and I wondered about how competent she was in an office of professional-looking people. And all of that from just her outfit.

I have also walked into businesses where the person serving me is dressed in such a way that I feel confident that he or she can help with what I need, even before they've said hello!

Like it or not, we judge and are judged by the bits of cloth and leather and fluff that we drape our bodies with ... all the time.

Just look at the "Best Dressed" and "Worst Dressed" pages of the fashion magazines. We judge a person on many levels based on what they put on that day.

You might be thinking, "But Jenn, I am an awesome person, and it's what's inside that counts and I don't care what anyone else thinks. I know how to do my job and that's what is important."

Yes, and sadly, no.

It is trivial and superficial to judge a person based on clothing or how many tattoos or piercings they have, or what colour their hair is this week. I agree completely and try very hard to catch myself anytime I find myself doing it. But the truth is it happens. A lot.

Is it fair? No.

Is it a reality? Yes.

Is it always the case? Thankfully not, but it happens enough that it is something to pay attention to when you want to create a great impression.

A LITTLE EXPERIMENT

If you want to experience this first-hand, try this exercise:[5]

1. Get dressed as if you are going to the gym or hanging out at home in your scruffies. Don't do much with your hair, and if you usually wear makeup or aftershave, don't. Stick a hat on your head or just wake up and go out without doing anything. Try it. I dare you to!
2. Go to a retail store or another business establishment such as a coffee shop or restaurant, and pay attention to how you are treated. Make some notes.
   a. Do people offer to help you?
   b. Are people friendly?
   c. Are they approaching you, or are they indifferent?
   d. How are people reacting to you?
   e. How are you feeling inside as you are noticing?
3. The next day (or later the same day), dress up. Get as fancy as you want. Get all business-looking or even dress as if you are going dancing.

---

[5] If you try my little clothing experiment as mentioned above, send me an email or voice mail on the website, and let me know what happens. I'm always interested in hearing from you. jenn@communicationdiva.com

4. Go back to the very same place you went the first time, and make note of how you are treated this time. (Often, the difference is stunning!)
   a. Do you get more or less attention, or is it the same?
   b. Are people friendlier or more helpful?
   c. How do you feel inside now that you are paying attention to this?

In general, people seem to be treated better (more politely, with more friendliness and courtesy) the better dressed they are. My female students who have gone into stores with no makeup, wearing fleece pants and tops, and carrying backpacks have reported being followed around the store because the staff thought they might shoplift! Others have reported going into big swanky department stores all dressed up and getting lots of attention from sales staff, and then going back to the very same store the next day in casual or workout clothing, and getting little if any attention or help. Some were simply ignored. Same person, different outfit.

Seems ridiculous and wrong, right?

So ... what to do?

How to Dress for Success

Some suggest an employee dress for the job he or she wants to have, rather than the job they do have. I understand this reasoning, and yet it is not always appropriate. You would look silly, for example, wearing a suit to work in a coffee shop, even if your dream was to own the franchise one day. Instead, I would suggest the following.

Know Your Working Environment

If you are working in a game-development company, the environment might be very different from that of a law office. Consider your physical setting: Is your workplace corporate, industrial, institutional, service, or retail, to name a few? What are others wearing? Do you see formal wear, business, business-casual, or casual clothing on your co-workers? What activities will you be doing in your work? Are you sitting down, moving about, driving a lot, making presentations, lifting heavy objects, or cleaning up after people? Often the environment itself will offer indicators of what will and will not be suitable to wear.

Know What the Dress Code Is

The dress code in your workplace could include anything from a scent policy (whether or not you can wear scented aftershave or perfume) to what safety equipment is required (ear protection, safety glasses, gloves, steel-toed boots, sturdy shoes, etc.). Some workplaces require uniforms, overalls, particular colour schemes, or business attire (e.g. suits and ties for men). The answer to "what to wear?" depends on your work environment. If you are unsure what is acceptable, ask.

Know Your Audience

Who are you dressing for? Knowing who you will be interacting with throughout your day will help you determine how you need to dress. Are you in customer service? Are you working in a warehouse, a film studio, or a legal office?

Are you indoors or outside? Do you work alone, or as part of a team? What messages would you like to send to those you are interacting with every day? These are questions to consider when deciding what to take from your closet each day.

The key thing to remember is that the messages your clothing sends others can undermine your professionalism if not in line with the work that you do. For example, I want my personal trainer to be dressed in workout clothes. This way, I know she is active, serious about fitness, and motivated to help get me moving. I want my mechanic to have greasy hands and to wear coveralls, otherwise I might wonder if he is actually the person doing the work on my vehicle. I want my doctor to be dressed in business clothing in her office. This shows respect for me as a patient, helps me feel confident in her medical abilities, and enables me to trust her recommendations. I want the judge in the courtroom to be in his official robes to convey how seriously he takes his decision-making, and I want the lab technician taking my blood to be in a clean uniform so that I can be confident she will follow proper phlebotomy protocol and take my blood safely and efficiently.

Clothing does not have anything to do with your actual skills, knowledge, abilities, or competence, and yet it has everything to do with other peoples' perceptions of them. You have the opportunity to create the messages you want to send by choosing wisely.

WHAT TO WEAR

CLOTHING

Once you understand the environment you will be working in, the dress code requirements and audience or customer you will be dealing with, then finding appropriate clothing should be easy. Being dressed in the latest fashion is nice, but not necessary unless you work in an industry that requires you to dress that way.

Try to avoid fads and funky fashion statements unless your workplace suits them. Being professional doesn't mean being boring or that you need to look like everyone else. You can certainly project a professional image with style.

When considering what to wear, be sure it is safe for your work environment, appropriate to the setting you are in, and remember that it is also about communication. That being said, be sure that what you do choose is clean, relatively wrinkle-free, and in good repair, because wrinkled, dirty, torn, or frayed clothing communicates that you don't care, which won't help further your aura of competence.

Also be careful of messages on clothing. Words, logos, brand names, and images that don't fit with the ethos of the company you work for will not be helpful. Save those for days off.

Be mindful of dress code expectations when travelling to other countries, especially if you are travelling on business. Research this before you go, so that you aren't caught by surprise. You might offend people from other cultures without knowing it by what you are or are not wearing, and that would not help you in your business transactions. How you dress does matter.

FOOTWEAR

Workplace policy and insurance rules might dictate that you wear footwear such as steel-toed boots, closed-toed, rubber-soled shoes, or other footwear suited to your work environment. Check the rules for your workplace, and then match the footwear to the rest of your attire. Athletic shoes, for example, with a business suit might be fine for the rainy bus ride to the office, but will look a little strange when meeting with your clients in the office to sign the papers for their new mortgage.

HATS

In some workplace environments, hats are essential and are part of the safety equipment required. Hard hats, helmets, and sun protection are often expected in jobs that involve construction and weather conditions. In more formal or business settings, hats and headwear are usually not appropriate, unless worn for religious or cultural purposes (or unless it's Crazy-Hat Day, in which case, go to town!). And again, if you travel for your work, take the time to find out what is and isn't culturally acceptable in the place you are going to so that you are not committing a dress code "faux pas."

ACCESSORIES

Tasteful accessorizing can enhance your look and give you a professional polish. The rule of thumb with this in most situations is that "less is more." Make-up, jewellery, hairstyle, and so on need to come under the same communication category as your clothing does: it will all send a message to others and, therefore, needs an investment of time and thought around exactly what message you intend to send.

Some companies have set policies on the topic. The Walt Disney Company, for example, has a long list of what is and isn't acceptable while working for their brand. Visible tattoos and piercings are still taboo in their regulations, while tidy beards and short moustaches have just recently been allowed.

If you work in a hair salon, you will have more room to get wild with styles and colours than you might in an insurance office. If you work in a body-piercing shop, then lip rings and earlobe expanders would be appropriate and likely expected. If you have a facial or visible body piercing and wonder about it, remove it during work hours if you can, at least until you can either ask your employer, or until you get a sense of whether or not you can wear it and still feel professional in your particular circumstance. The same goes with tattoos. If you don't know, cover your ink up, until you are clear about what is allowed or acceptable.

LOOKING GOOD DOESN'T HAVE TO BE EXPENSIVE

It is completely possible to dress well for work without breaking the bank. I am a big fan of consignment stores and thrift-store shopping, both from an environmental standpoint, and from an expense perspective. I have found exceedingly chic pieces of dress clothing for work at a fraction of the cost of buying new, and part of the fun for me is "the thrill of the chase"!

You might find wearing other peoples' discards distasteful,

which is too bad (you can wash and dry-clean things, you know), but if you are not willing to shop used, then most stores have end-of-season sales, and business dress clothing is often classic and doesn't go out of style quickly, so can be acquired at the end of one season in preparation for the next. There are also programs in many cities that offer business clothing to people who need some help financially to get a wardrobe going. Often these can be accessed through government employment programs.

PERSONAL HYGIENE: HAVE YOU BRUSHED YOUR HAIR LATELY?

Not looking after your personal hygiene will not only scream out a nonverbal message that you don't care about yourself or those you work with, but might actually prevent you from getting to know your co-workers. If you smell bad, for example, people will avoid you. If you look unkempt, assumptions will be made about your character. Keeping yourself clean, well-groomed, and approachable sends a positive message to the world. Remember that impression is based on perception, which then leads to what people believe about you. The more opportunity you give people to get a good impression of you, the better!

A FINAL NOTE ON APPEARANCE

A group of researchers headed by Jeremy C. Biesanz at the University of British Columbia, Department of Psychology, did a study asking whether or not people have insight into how accurate their first impressions of others are. After setting up two interactive sessions where people met each other in pairs for a short while (think speed dating), the researchers noted that there are two ways to be accurate about the initial impressions made: we can recognize the differences and the similarities. It turns out that those who recognized similarities in themselves were more accurate. Most people are somewhat alike or could be considered "typical." For example, most people in an interview setting want to be liked and will be friendly toward their interviewer instead of argumentative. The more typical and similar the subject was to the person interacting with them, the more accurate the person felt their impression was. When compared to the perceptions of people who actually knew the subject (friends and family), those who felt strongly that they were accurate, actually were. "Many important decisions are made after very brief encounters—which job candidate to hire, which person to date, which student to accept," write the authors of the study. "Although our first impressions are generally accurate, it is critical for us to recognize when they may be lacking."[6]

The good news is that you have the ability to use this often-overlooked form of nonverbal communication (your clothing) to your advantage. To appear confident, competent, successful, and professional in your job, take time and care with how you look ... *it does* make a difference.

---

[6] J.C. Biesanz, L. J. Human, A.C. Paquin, M. Chan, K. L. Parisotto, J. Sarracino, and R. L. Gillis. "Do We Know When Our Impressions of Others Are Valid? Evidence for Realistic Accuracy Awareness in First Impressions of Personality." *Social Psychological and Personality Science*, 2011

Chapter Four

Nonverbal Cues—It's Not All About What You Say

Paralanguage—Everything But the Words

Your voice is a unique expression of who you are. It is of course, a huge part of how you say something that distinguishes you from everyone else. (Think: voice recognition technology.) How you use your voice can make a difference to how you come across to others. While words are really important (there are definitely better ways than others to say things), the words are not as important as what happens around them. Paralanguage is the fancy word for everything around the actual word itself. "Para" means around or beside and "language" refers to the words.

Paralanguage includes:

- the tone and pitch of your voice
- the speed of your speech
- hesitation noises, like "ummm" or "ahhhh"
- facial expressions made while saying words

Just changing these elements can change the whole communication, even when you are saying the exact same words. Here's an example.

Try saying "Hey, Taylor, let's go." with the instructions listed:

- Say it sadly.
- Say it with anger.
- Say it suggestively.
- Say it excitedly.
- Say it while yawning or stretching.
- Say it with slurred speech.

Each time you say the very same sentence but with the change in your paralanguage, the meaning changes. There also is not just one particular interpretation of the final message. Saying the sentence while yawning, for example, could mean you are either sleepy or bored ... two distinct messages.

You can see that paralanguage is tricky stuff!

Have you ever said something to someone and had that person then ask you, "Why did you say it like *that*?"

It could be that you said words that meant one thing, but the paralanguage you used sent another message entirely. When these things don't line up, when they are incongruent, the person on the receiving end gets a mixed message ... and is often confused. This is often the source of conflict, because if you just let it go and don't bother to check in with how the message was received, then the other person is going to go away upset. Having someone leave a conversation upset or confused by your mixed message is never a good thing, because it usually means that someone in the conversation **wasn't** being:

- clear
- patient
- a good listener
- honest

If you say something without really meaning it, often it will show ... maybe not on your face if you are good at acting, but often in the subtleties of your tone or pitch or rate of speech.

Paralanguage is powerful and worth paying attention to.

How many times have you asked someone if they want to do something, they say yes, but you get the overwhelming sense they don't actually mean it? That happens a lot. For whatever reason, instead of being authentic and *honest*, the person says something he or she doesn't actually mean, and then spends time, after the fact, grumbling about having to do it, whatever "it" is.

Then, there are the stock responses that annoy me, especially when I hear myself giving them. You know, the "How are you today?" response that is typically "Fine, thanks," or "Good, thanks," or if you want to be grammatically correct, "I'm well, thank-you." Now, it may be that you are being completely honest in this mundane response. Maybe you *are* fine or good or well.

Often this "rote" form of greeting sounds insincere. Does the person asking *really* care how you are, or are they asking because it's a standard greeting? Are they even looking you in the eye when the greeting is made? And what happens next? Are they going to listen to you if you don't happen to be okay?

If it's a case of asking the question because they feel they need to say something, then sometimes I will answer with the standard response. However, if I want to see if they truly are listening, I will often say something like:

"I'm really hungry right now. How 'bout you?"

or

"I'm not really sure right at the moment; it's been a long day."

or

"I'm super tired."

Or any number of other responses that are more interesting than the stock ones.

This unexpected, non-stock response does two things:

- It usually wakes the other person out of the mundane blather that we mumble to each other by rote or mindlessly as we transact with one another.
- It brings on an actual mini-conversation and, depending on where you happen to be and who you are talking with, this mini-conversation could possibly lead to a longer one that actually has meaning.

Listen to how the standard question is asked of you. Listen to the paralanguage. You'll learn more about whether the person asking is being genuine or not, or if they are just going through the motions.

In coaching circles, listening to paralanguage is called Level 2 listening or listening beyond words.[7] As a brand new employee, it is a great idea to listen beyond words to what's happening around you, and to what people want

---

[7]There is Level 3 listening as well that incorporates listening to the paralanguage, but goes beyond that to watching for body language including gestures and slight movements, energy levels, and emotional responses such as facial flushing, and more. It involves intuition and listening to the person in a holistic way.

from you. If you wonder about something that is said with a tone of voice that sounds funny to you given the words spoken, the very best communication tool you can ever use is ... wait for it ... **curiosity!**

Just ask. It will save you hours of worrying and crying in your cereal if you just ask if something isn't right. Use something like "I'm picking up that you aren't happy with something I've just said; can I ask about that?"

Or whatever language works for you. The idea is to get curious and be straightforward and assertive about checking your gut instinct in the moment. If you think what you said was misinterpreted, then ask about it. That will save all sorts of angst and fuss later.

We'll talk more about curiosity in future chapters, but for now, simply notice the paralanguage that's happening in your next conversation with an unsuspecting person. He or she doesn't need to know what you are doing. It can be your own little exercise in becoming a better communicator.

A Poem

Because I love to communicate, and because some things people say and do just make me crazy, I wrote this piece back in 2010 for a youth, open-mic night that I was part of at a coffee house. It's a post that is looked at almost daily on my site.

This poem is meant to be read in a rhythmic tone and to be performed, so if you are reading it in your head, imagine someone performing it ... it'll just be better. Trust me.

Just Fine

Fine thanks, she said in response to my question
and carried on past me fast
not wanting to engage
or open to the page
of her particular book of life ...
somebody's wife ...
with lines of heartache on her pretty face,
which only renewed passion could erase,
but she wouldn't divulge.
"Just fine," said she.
F-I-N-E
Feelings Inside, Never Expressed.
It's the answer we give,
the one we like best,
when not wanting to reveal what's
under the peel of the onion's layer.
"Fine" is safe.
Safe in this world of internet spies and electronic eyes,
surfing into our business,
stealing our is-ness.
But everything is just fine
if drowned in wine or soaked in gold.
And there's always a way to litigate,
or medicate ... or at least mitigate with therapy:
- massage therapy
- psychotherapy
- aromatherapy
- spiritual therapy
- retail therapy!
It all costs a bundle,

which is why we trundle on
to work ... where different demons lurk.
But at least we're being productive, which
is far more seductive
than holy leisure on a resume!
We trod the boards,
alone in hordes ...
Don't Talk!
Don't Share!
Don't let anyone in ...
Don't you see? I'm
F-I-N-E.
A universal chorus it seems that
suddenly screams,
"INDIVIDUALISM IS MY SHIELD !!!"
Don't come near ... I live in fear
that someone might see
my vulnerability ...
and that ... would be bad.
"Just fine," she said, eyes quite dead,
soul depleted ...
feet receding down the hallway
of lame answers.
Conversation Over.

SPATIAL COMMUNICATION

CLOSE TALKERS, PERSONAL BUBBLES, HALITOSIS, AND HAPPY THOUGHTS

How you use the space around you in nonverbal communication, and how close or far you get from another person

when communicating with them are elements of the sub-category of nonverbal communication called "proxemics." The use of space can add to or subtract from a person's overall professional aura, and is something few people take time to consider. Each of us has a space around us (a personal bubble) that we "own" or protect. For some, this is a very small space, and so standing very close to someone when speaking to them is normal, comfortable, and what they do. For others, getting that close gets really uncomfortable, and unless they back up and give themselves the space, they feel (as my mother likes to say) "antsy." Uncomfortable. Each of us also manages the space we work in in different ways. I've seen people put signs on office chairs indicating they were only to be used by certain people; in other words, the chairs were "reserved space." I've been known to label a clipboard on the job so that only I was invited to use it. Some people unofficially "lay claim" to a particular parking spot at work. When you share space with another person in your workplace setting, such as a lunchroom, a refrigerator, a closet to hang coats in, or perhaps even a desk, work station, service bay, or office, how do you treat that space? Do you leave things strewn all over it? Are you careful to respect the property of others, or do you take up an entire shelf in the fridge with your large sac-o'-lunch fixings? What you do with your space and the space of others communicates something. Pay attention to shared space and how you treat it. Be aware of the messages you might potentially send by your use of space in communication (unintentionally or otherwise) as doing so can go a very long way to how people perceive you.

An Exercise in Spatial Awareness

I do an exercise in my classroom that brings awareness to the students about their own tolerances for having other people in their personal space, and that also demonstrates the differences in individual tolerances in a very visual way.

I line up six students shoulder to shoulder at one end of the room facing the opposite wall. Then I have six more students line up the same way along that opposite wall, facing the first six.

I have the first group of students remain stationary and, on my cue, the second group begins to walk slowly toward the stationary group. They are to maintain constant eye contact with the person they are heading toward as they move. Whenever the person who is standing still starts to feel uncomfortable with the nearness of the approaching person, she or he can put up a hand and the walking person has to stop.

Once everyone has stopped, I ask them to stay where they are and to look around and notice what they see. We look at the differences in where each of the walking people have been stopped. Some are almost nose-to-nose with the person standing still. Others are several feet back. Some are in various locations in between.

I ask the people who stood still how they felt about the exercise. Then I ask the walking people how they felt, and some of them (those who didn't have a chance to stop because the person they were walking toward didn't put up a hand to stop them) say they felt really uncomfortable being as close as they were allowed to get. We then try the exercise again and I have the people who were stationary do the walking, noticing more differences in the results when the roles are switched.

It's an interesting exercise in spatial awareness, and is a

very good way to realize how uncomfortable some people feel when others get too close.

The ability to control how close people get to you goes right out the window on a bus or in a subway when you have to be jammed up against people. But in normal circumstances, being aware of your own comfort level (how close you want to get to people when interacting with them), and also being aware that your personal bubble might be really different from someone else's is a good thing to recognize.

As demonstrated repeatedly in my classroom exercises, some people (generally the ones who get right up close and personal), are completely unaware of how uncomfortable they are making the person they are talking to feel. It's particularly bad if these people ate delicious yet nasty-smelling things and have halitosis. Or if they forgot to brush their teeth and you are staring at their leftover breakfast.

Here's how to tell if how close you are to someone else is making them feel nervous:

- They back up.
- They cross their arms and lean back.
- They turn away.
- They completely stiffen.
- They ask you to back off.

The last one shouldn't have to happen, but if the person is assertive enough to do it, then good for them! Otherwise, paying attention to the clues and cues a person is sending to you nonverbally, and being sure not to get too close to them the next time would be good. Getting into another person's personal space when unwanted can ruin a relationship.

NONVERBAL MESSAGING

There is some debate about what percentage of human communication is verbal and what percentage is nonverbal. Some say our nonverbal communication makes up 75 percent of all the messages we send, while others say it's much higher. Being aware that the majority of what you communicate comes from your nonverbal messaging can help you to be sure to send the messages you want to send.

There are many ways to say something without using words, and it is likely that you have done this. A person can have an entire conversation with another person without speaking. In fact, if you are a Mr. Bean fan, you will know that entire movies can be made without words!

A subtle raise of an eyebrow can communicate you are surprised or that you question what the other is saying. Crossed arms can indicate an unwillingness to be approached, or can simply mean the room temperature is colder than comfortable.

The person in the elevator next to you yawns. You smile and they smile back at you. You sigh and nod in a knowing way because you feel tired too, and it would have been nice to have stayed in bed a little longer. A complete conversation can happen through body language without ever saying a word.

So How Can Knowing This Information Be Helpful?

Actions scream louder than words in many instances and, because they do, it is a good idea to think about this for a minute. If **most** of what you communicate is not through your mouth using words, then what messages are you sending? We're going to explore some of these in the coming chapters, but right now I want to focus on things you might be doing that you don't even know you are doing. These are the things that can get us into trouble.

Nonverbal Movements

Ekman and Friesen developed five categories of nonverbal movement in 1969 that are still widely used today by sociologists.[8] The categories have fancy technical names, and yet are groupings of movements that you will likely be very familiar with. Let's look at each one and list some of the possible messages you might be inadvertently sending.

1. Emblem Movements

These are gestures so commonly understood and widely used that we have words in the English language to explain them. "Wink" or "smile" for example. No words need be exchanged when using an emblem movement, unless there is the possibility of misinterpretation. A "high-five" movement means congratulations are being shared. A smile, for example, usually means you are happy or glad

---

[8]Ekman, P.; Friesen, W.V. (1971). "Constants across cultures in the face and emotion." *Journal of Personality and Social Psychology* 17: 124–129.

about something. If you smile when you hear something sad or upsetting or when being given negative feedback at work, however, you could unintentionally be sending the wrong message, even though a smile is often simply a nervous reaction. Perhaps you are busy thinking about your delicious bagged lunch when someone tells you a sad story, and you suddenly realize you have stopped listening and are smiling inappropriately. Another example is the wink. A wink is usually meant to be supportive, sweet, or cute. Often people who do this habitually don't even realize it. Sometimes, it can be seen as suggestive, which is definitely not appropriate for the workplace.

Make sure your emblem movements match the messages you want to send. And think before you wink!

2. Illustrator Movements

These are movements that aren't used to replace words, but to enhance or illustrate them. You might be describing the stack of work you still have to tackle on your desk and you use your hands to show how tall it is. You might want to illustrate with hand movements a concept you are presenting in a meeting. These can be useful gestures, and often we do them unconsciously. Problems arise, however, when these movements are misread. For example, you might roll your eyes a lot. This might be an unconscious movement. It might be a nervous tic. You might have Tourette Syndrome.[9] It might be that you are thinking that whatever

---

[9]I'm not being funny here. Tourette's runs in my family. My half-brother, son, and nephew all have it. My son was once complimented on how he added so much to an onstage performance as a sleazy game-show host character by repeatedly making what looked like a sassy little chin-nod movement. I didn't have the heart to explain to the woman doing the complimenting that the movement was actually part of the syndrome, and that he was just making it work for him as an actor. He's a super-smart guy that way.

the person is saying or doing is ridiculous, and while you aren't verbally saying a thing, you are unaware that you are practically yelling it with your eyes. Again, paying attention to what your facial features are doing to illustrate or embellish your thoughts and words is a start. You might want to develop your "poker face"!

3. Affect Display

These are actions or gestures that match your emotions. Perhaps you are pulling a lost lunch bag out of the staff refrigerator and are scrunching up your face in disgust as you realize it's been there for weeks and smells. Anyone looking at your face would know you were feeling disgust. Raising eyebrows could mean you are feeling surprise, shock, disbelief, disapproval, aggression, or attraction. Blushing could indicate embarrassment, shame, feeling flattered, stress, attraction, or could indicate physiological symptoms such as overheating from a workout, sunburn, or menopause. If you want to keep your emotional responses to yourself in a work situation, pay close attention to your affect displays, particularly the ones you can control.

4. Regulator Movements

This category of nonverbal gestures is especially important in the workplace. Examples include nodding to encourage someone, smiling to let someone know you see them, the handshake, eye contact to indicate you are listening or are willing to listen, and what are called "minimal encouragers," which are small noises such as "uh-huh," "mmm," or "ah" that are used to keep conversation flowing. Failure to express regulator movements can be a problem because you might appear unengaged or disinterested. Regulator movements allow the other person who is talking to know that you are listening and interested in what they are saying and are willing to connect. Check out your skill with regulator movements the next time you are listening to another person speak in a conversation or a business presentation. It is likely you make them quite naturally. Once you are conscious of them, notice what effect they have on the person you are interacting with. It can be quite revealing.

5. Adaptor Actions

These are the ones that can get us into the most trouble, as they are unconscious habits or movements often intended to fix bodily discomfort: yawning, sniffing, twirling or sucking on your hair, scratching an itch, shifting weight, fidgeting, nail-biting, toe-tapping, etc. These can be seen as signs of nervousness, agitation, anxiety, or ennui, and can often be interpreted incorrectly by someone observing them.

Is that yawn because you are bored of the subject of my presentation? Or is it because you stayed up half the night trying to beat the game level you were on?

Either way, the message you could be sending might be negative, and can easily be changed once you are aware of what you are doing.

Some other nonverbal movements that could send messages you don't intend to send are as follows:

1. You touch people when you talk to them.
2. You slouch when sitting, or lean (sprawl or lounge) across your desk.

3. You drift off daydreaming when someone is talking to you.
4. You don't smile much.
5. You cross your arms or use closed body language frequently.

Be mindful of cultural differences around touching. Some cultures are much more hands off and others are much more hands-on. In North America, we tend to shake hands as a business greeting, a sign of agreeing to a transaction, and when saying goodbye. This works, unless the person you are dealing with is from a culture that doesn't shake hands and is uncomfortable with it. It is more professional to pay attention to the nonverbal cues the other person might be sending you. If they stand back and don't make the hand-coming-at-you move, then that's a clue. If they swoop in and hug you ... you might be the one who is uncomfortable! I find it weird to hug someone I've never met before (although I've done it), and I found it even weirder to be kissed on each cheek once when meeting someone for the very first time.[10] It wasn't unbearable or anything, it just surprised me for a moment, because it's not what I'm culturally used to.

I once hugged a person who, I remembered too late from the far recesses of my brain, didn't like to be hugged. She just stood there like a wooden board, enduring what turned into a very quick, very awkward, and rather apologetic sort of hug. I have remembered ever since never to hug this woman, because she doesn't feel comfortable being hugged. And I really don't believe in inflicting my desire

---

[10]This happened to me when I was in Paris. While it is not an unusual greeting in France, I just wasn't expecting it, and when a stranger aims at your face with theirs, it can be a little startling!

to hug people on those who find the action excruciatingly uncomfortable. I met someone once who hugs absolutely everyone he meets regardless of whether or not they want to be hugged, and he gleefully announces to anyone who will listen that no matter what other people say, everyone "could use a hug." While I understand that he thinks he is doing something good, I also know that he is being really disrespectful of other people and imposing his own beliefs on them, which is fairly aggressive behaviour, if you think about it.

My suggestion again would be to pay attention to what *you* do, and also to how the other person reacts to what you do, because you can learn a lot from that, both about yourself and about the other person. You might be inadvertently communicating something you actually don't intend to.[11] The good thing is that once you notice what it is you are doing, you can be in full control of it and send the nonverbal messages you want to send.

What Your Stuff Says About You

Your Personal Things and How You Keep Them

The things you keep on your desk say something to the world. You might think it's just a chipped coffee mug your sister brought you back from Disneyland eight years ago, but in a professional setting, the silent message you send by having it there might indicate another message, such as

---

[11] I know I keep saying "pay attention" to this and that, and you might wonder how you are supposed to think of all of these things at once. My answer is, you aren't. Choose one thing you'd like to work on at a time and make it your goal to pay attention to that one thing. Then move on when you are ready.

lack of care (it's damaged) and lack of style (tourist ware instead of sleek and modern mugs for the office), and its presence could detract from your overall professional and polished look, and that of your workplace.

Your "stuff" is a form of communication.

How much stuff, what kind of stuff, and what you do with your stuff all speaks volumes.

If you have a passion for a particular hobby or design, this might translate into the things you keep in your workspace. Same goes if you are a collector.

This can work for or against you, depending on where you work, and what kind of message you want to send.

I have a friend who loves shoes. She has all sorts of office equipment (staplers, business card holders, pen and pencil holders, you name it) in the shape of shoes. She's easy to buy for, because she loves all that stuff, and anyone approaching her desk, even if they've never met her, will know that she is a shoe-fanatic. Or perhaps I should say, enthusiast.

She is working in an environment where her friendliness and approachability are key, and sharing her passion with the world makes people smile and makes them feel like they can talk to her, even before they meet her. In this case, it works to have this kind of decor, and it gives people something to talk about with her.

My kids had a teacher who adored apples. Everything on her desk, from her clock to her Mac computer, had to do with apples. The children gave her gifts at the end of the year that had to do with apples. Again, this was a form of communication. She even assigned the same "apple project" to every class she taught and the children came to expect apple stickers on returned assignments. The apple was her signature statement.

It's good to notice how the objects you keep around you speak to others, and what messages you are sending through them. If you want to send a message about efficiency, professionalism, and reliability, think carefully and choose your desk-decor wisely. This doesn't mean it has to be boring by any means. You can be very artsy and chic while sending a professional message. Be careful of being too "cutesy," unless your work environment lends itself to that.

Family photos, items that represent hobbies you enjoy (like a framed map of your favourite place to scuba dive) are okay to have in your workspace as long as you want people around you to know what it is that you value, and as long as your workplace allows it. These things on your desk or in your workspace can actually be a great way to communicate with your peers, clients, or superiors, and can be really good conversation-starters, especially if the items are displayed in a tasteful and appropriate way.

I was recently at a physician's office where the walls were covered with beautiful framed photographs of places around the world, all taken by the physician himself. This mini art gallery told me the doctor was well-travelled, adventurous, and talented in more ways that just "doctoring." I thought it was far more interesting to have these pieces on the walls than some of the other office waiting room decor I've seen, and it gave me a new perspective on the man in the white coat.

You could actually plan this kind of communication. It might even be fun.

While the following section refers to dressing your "desk," the same principles apply to any work area you might be in that can house some of your personal belongings. You may only have space to carry a lunch kit, or to pin up a favourite photo, and even those limited items will convey messages to those who see them.

How to Dress Your Desk

First, consider your new environment:

- What kind of business is it?
- What is the tone of the work environment: is it playful, casual, formal, or serious? This can help to guide you in your decor choices.
- How much "customizing" are you even allowed to do with your space?
- What do you want people to know about you?

This is similar to what you considered when choosing what clothing to wear. Once you have answers, **dress your "desk"** with items and decor that will send the message you want to send to anyone who enters your workspace.

How You Keep Your Things

A tidy workspace communicates organization, care, and respect of both self and others. It also appears professional. If the hand tools in a woodworking shop are hung neatly on wall pegs and organized in labelled drawers, the stacks of wood neatly placed on shelves, and the sawdust cleaned up off the floor, a client will get a message that the craftsperson is creative, competent, and capable of producing something beautiful.

If your space needs help, there are ways to convey

orderliness. If you are at a desk or in an office setting, you can use file organizers, in and out baskets, nice decorative boxes with lids that keep things looking neat even if they aren't, and you can stack things in a tidy fashion (use storage bins or shelving), which can make a workspace look more efficient. If your space looks more efficient, guess what? So do you.

You also will appear to be:

- organized
- responsible
- able to manage your time
- able to keep up with the workload
- caring and committed to your job

People receive messages simply by walking past your workspace. A clean and tidy work area sends the "I am a professional" message.

CELL PHONES

It's easy to say to someone, "Don't be attached to your cell phone." But I know personally that I am, *and* I know that I don't need to be attached to it at work.

Where Is Your Phone?

Company policy may dictate if and when you can have your cell phone with you in your workspace. If there is no set policy, and unless you use your cellphone for business purposes, put it on vibrate in your drawer, your pocket, your briefcase, or your work bag, and leave it there until you take your coffee-break or lunch. The constant distraction of checking for texts or emails or answering calls will both interrupt the work you are supposed to be doing, and could be dangerous to you or others depending on your work environment. Having your attention turned repeatedly to your device, particularly when not in the line of duty, is also noticeably unprofessional behaviour. Instead, be present, focussed, and engaged in the work you are paid to do, and you will shine.

Ringtones

Custom ringtones can be fun. (I had "Jump" by Van Halen as mine once.) Ringtones are also a form of nonverbal communication that say something about who you are. If you have your cell phone on for work purposes, be sure your ringtone is something you want others to hear, or better yet, set the cell to vibrate.

Headphones, Music, and More

If you are a 911 Operator, a receptionist, a telemarketer, or a Medical Transcriptionist, then headsets are an essential part of your working equipment. If you work where you need to have protective gear to prevent hearing loss, then you will have earmuffs on, and whether or not you are permitted to also have music playing through ear buds under your earmuffs is something to confirm. In some settings, this combination would be a safety hazard. Check the company policy about listening to music with headphones for your particular situation. Some workplaces allow employees to listen to music while working, as it can reduce stress and distraction, and increase productivity.

WHAT'S THAT SMELL?

Many workplaces discourage food and drink in work-spaces, particularly if you have expensive computers and equipment you're working with, or if you are in an enclosed place where others might have life-threatening allergies and could react to the peanuts you are eating next to them. With the exception of water, having food and beverages in your workspace is messy, unprofessional, and might even be dangerous.[12] If you are dealing with customers, chewing, munching, or slurping while talking to them won't be impressive. Neither will spilling coffee down your front, or being caught with your mouth full when answering the phone. Save the snacking for the lunchroom, and keep your work area tidy and crumb-free.

Professionalism is conveyed by how you conduct yourself *all the time.*

CHEWING GUM

Some people love to chew gum and this is something I have no issue with in a non-work setting. But in the workplace, especially in a customer-service setting where you are interacting with people face to face, chewing gum is inappropriate and can be offensive to some people. Some companies actually forbid it.

---

[12]Distracted driving is dangerous, and eating in your work truck while on the road may not yet be illegal, but could be dangerous. So could spilling liquids on electronic equipment in a lab, or tipping hot coffee over onto someone next to you. If you are working with chemicals, you wouldn't want food in the same space. Open food in a hospital nursing station is also unsafe with all the germs present in patient care areas.

I was at the bank waiting to see my banker, when I noticed one of the tellers, a lovely young woman dressed in business clothes, serving a customer at her window. What I noticed was that she was chomping away on her gum while serving the customer. She was talking and chewing at the same time, and that small bit of gum instantly destroyed her otherwise professional appearance.

Sue Morem, author of *How to Gain the Professional Edge* and columnist at careerknowhow.com says, "Chewing gum is unprofessional." She goes on to say, "Don't be too hard on the gum chewers you meet; everyone has imperfections and idiosyncrasies. We all ... should be more aware of our habits and our affect on others."[13]

I would have to agree and add that the little things—idiosyncrasies and habits—add up to big things and that, sometimes, it's a series of these little things that give someone the impression of you that they walk away with and keep.

What Is on Your Computer Screen?

People walk past your desk and are often able to see what you are looking at or working on. What they see on your screen is a form of communication. It is important as an employee to know what your company expects on this topic, and to use the same discretion and attention to environment as you did when dressing your body or your workspace. Let's talk first about desktop graphics and then discuss social media.

---

[13]Sue Morem, suemorem.com, from her "Ask Sue" Column About Professionalism, Etiquette, and Problems in the Workplace. www.careerknowhow.com/ask_sue/habits. htm [Accessed December 18, 2014]

SCREENSAVERS

Your screensaver and the image you choose as your desktop background say something about you. Fading to black is good ... it just looks like your screen is off, unless that's bad and makes it look like you aren't working at all. You might not be allowed to customize what shows up. It may be that policy says the company logo only must glow or glide across your screen.

If you are allowed to customize your screensaver, be sure whatever picture or design you choose fits with the image you want to project—family photos, a pet picture, an inspirational saying, a scene from somewhere you've been, or whatever you decide to use. Think about the ambience of the space you work in, and go with something that will fit.

The same goes for the desktop background image. Some companies require you to leave the desktop image alone. Others allow you to customize it. Again, think twice before using pictures of bikini-clad beach beauties or your personal party pictures, because these send messages that are not professional. So, too, does a large collection of cute baby pictures. Think about dressing your virtual desk with a clear and positive message about you.

SOCIAL MEDIA MAYHEM

This is a very large and very controversial topic in many office circles. Some companies turn a blind eye and go with the theory that a few minutes of a "social media brain break" makes for a more productive employee. (I tend to agree with this, but I'm not the boss.)

Some companies want and expect their employees to be

interacting with clients and others on social media as part of their job, and if that's the case, then what I'm about to say doesn't apply.

Some companies monitor exactly what employees look at on their computers at work and even restrict access. Prisons, for example, have very strict internet settings for employees for security reasons. Many companies restrict access to the internet to prevent or limit exposure to computer viruses. Others limit employee access to prevent personal use during paid working hours.

Either way, this can be a good or a bad thing, depending on what you do.

Find out what the rules and policies are in your workplace so you know what you can or cannot do.

Here are some general guidelines:

Be Mindful of What Internet Sites You Visit

Often on the job, what you look at and *how long* you look at it is recorded, and this information is kept for future reference. Whether you are climbing the corporate ladder, looking for job references, moving to a new position, or are heading into an employee performance review, the history of your internet access is part of your employee record. It may be funny to share questionable joke videos with your co-workers now, but you could seriously regret it down the road. Other site surfing might also be frowned upon, such as viewing non-work-related shopping or entertainment sites, or checking out your company's competition.

I was working at a hospital when a co-worker called to tell me she'd just been reprimanded by her supervisor because she had sent a union-related email from her workspace computer. She'd sent it only moments before to a small group of union reps, and somehow, management found out. She was told she had to send such communications from her home computer or from a union office computer and only on her own time, not when at work. Her phone call to me was mostly to tell me how surprised she was that *they* were actually monitoring employee emails, and that nothing we did electronically at work was actually private.

Good to know.

I don't know of any organization that would tolerate employees looking at pornographic or hate-based sites. Doing so on the job is completely unacceptable.

My advice, to help you stand out and shine and be professional, is to limit social media and personal internet activity on the job in general. Unless use of social media platforms is part of your job, save your updates for coffee time if you must be in touch. It's best to look at your favourite pop star's fan page on your personal device during your lunch break, or better yet, save it for the transit ride home.

What You Do at Home Might Come Back to Haunt You

Chances are, when you applied for the job, your social media presence was investigated. Someone went onto your

Facebook profile, your LinkedIn profile, checked Twitter, Instagram, and Google Plus, or any number of other places you might hang out.

Why? Lots of reasons. This is where they can see what you are looking at, what you're interested in, who your friends are, what kind of language you use, what groups you belong to, and more. What you post on social media platforms **never** (ever) goes away, and so that nasty comment you made six months ago on Facebook is still there. It could even be a positive comment you made but using non-workplace language. For example, that enthusiastic expletive you dropped on your brother's page when you saw a picture of his brand new shiny pickup truck with all the options is still there.

People have been fired for things said and sites visited on the internet. You might think that what you look at and what sites you comment on is your own private business once you aren't at work, but that is only true to a point. If you are spewing out hateful or racist stuff, you might not be the kind of employee the company you are working for wants on board, and they might find any excuse to get rid of you. If you are sharing links related to topics that would not be viewed in a good light where you work, then it is entirely possible that someone who is looking up your public profile will find it.

Just try putting your own name into a search engine and see what comes up. You might be a little surprised.

A wise tip: If you don't want your grandma to read it, then don't post it.

Chapter Five

Verbal Communication

Verbal communication refers to the words used when speaking, the tone of voice used, and the rate of speech. While the words that we use when communicating with each other are only part of the entire communication, they are absolutely critical and can be hard to hear if the messages sent are not received correctly. Accusation, tone of voice, mumbling, or speaking too quickly, and lack of skill in listening can all impede the proper receiving of the message you are trying to send. In the next two chapters, we'll look at a few key elements of verbal communication that, once adopted, will bring you concrete results and make you a much better communicator.

Communication Basics: Three Key Skills

1. Use "I" Language

"I" language is a way of phrasing things that will let you talk about your take on a situation, without blaming, without using the very vague terms *they* and *some people*, and while sharing what it's like from your side of the boat.

Example: You want a co-worker to introduce you to new clients when they come into the office, so that you can get to know names and faces. You've asked them to do that.

It happened again that your co-worker didn't, so you approach him or her.

You could say something like this: "You didn't introduce me when that new client came in. I thought you were going to do that so I could get to know people."

Your co-worker's immediate first reaction could be defensive, because the above statement is basically an accusation. You didn't do something, and you said you would. This is an example of not using "I" language and setting yourself up for a potential conflict.

You could say something like this instead, making sure that the tone you use conveys that you are simply stating your feelings and not accusing the other person:

"I notice you didn't introduce me to that new client and I'm feeling frustrated, mostly I think because I want to get to know people here. I would appreciate it if next time a client comes in, you would remember to introduce me to them."

This second example is really wordy, takes longer to say, and you might need to put it into language that you would *actually* use, but the idea is that you are talking about yourself first, telling it like it is from your perspective without judging why the other person behaved the way they did. This technique takes some planning to make sure you are truly using "I" language and not just rearranging the words and still outright accusing them.

In this last example, you do the following:

- You name a behaviour you **notice.**
- You name how this behaviour **makes you feel**.
- You name **why you think** you feel this way.

- You **ask for a change** in the behaviour or for what you need the next time.

This is an exceedingly clear way of communicating, and "I" language does that. It allows you to say how you feel, what you noticed or saw or experienced, and what you'd like to happen another time. Instead of telling someone what they should and shouldn't do, you are letting them know how what they did or didn't do affected you, and what you need to have happen the next time. It is the act of reframing the message in a way that is easier for your co-worker to hear.

It also makes it difficult for the other person to argue with, because it is really hard to argue about how someone else feels.

Feelings are just that—feelings—and they have no right or wrong to them because they just exist. They just are. If you say, "I feel sad," it's rather hard to argue with that. Someone saying, "No, you don't" to your statement of sadness is highly unlikely. So if you say what you want to say from "your" perspective, share how "you" feel and ask for what "you" need, chances are your statement will be better received. No guarantees, of course, but beginning from your own experience is almost always the better plan.

2. PRACTISE ACTIVE LISTENING

You've probably heard about this one, because it's talked about a lot. Active listening means listening more than talking, being present while you listen,[14] and picking up on

---

[14] I don't mean physically being present, I mean actually being *in* the conversation in your mind and not off thinking about tonight's hot date. It takes a lot of work to stay present in the "now" and it's impossible all the time, but when it really counts, being fully present is critical.

subtle cues and things the other person is telling you with their paralanguage and their body language, and not just on the words they use. The Greek philosopher Diogenes said, "We have been given two ears and one tongue so that we may listen more and talk less." Doing this is a challenge for many, and often with good reason.

Here are some reasons why it can be hard to listen actively:

1. **You are preoccupied with something else.** Maybe you've got too much going on in your life. You are worrying about something or thinking about something else, even though your body is present and you might look like you are listening. The sure sign of not listening is when the person talking to you asks you something and you suddenly find that you have not been paying attention and have no idea what the person was talking about. Busted!

2. **There is too much noise.** Maybe you are in a loud environment, at a party, or in a crowded place with loud music, or on a construction site, or your barista is grinding the beans for that delicious French vanilla non-fat foamy latte you ordered ... and it's hard to hear. It can be challenging and frustrating and almost impossible to remain focussed on what someone is saying if you can't really even hear them.

3. **You have a lack of training.** Some people have never considered how well they listen (or don't listen) and this can present problems, because again, it's a skill and, as with any skill, it takes knowledge and practise. If you've never even thought about it, if you

don't pay attention to either your own listening skills or the skills of people you interact with, then chances are you could use some training and practice.

4. **There are heavy accent or language-skill issues.** Sometimes, it's really hard to understand someone if your ear isn't tuned in to their accent, or if they are not functionally able to speak your language. I ended up not ordering take-out from a restaurant once because the person on the other end of the phone could barely speak English, and I was trying to ask about my multiple food allergies so that I didn't end up in anaphylactic shock from eating the food I wanted to order. After an extremely frustrating several minutes of not being able to understand each other, I thanked the man, hung up, and called another restaurant. It wasn't worth the risk, and it wasn't that I wasn't ready to listen ... it was that even listening, I wasn't understanding.

5. **You assume what you know the person is going to say before they ever say it.** Sometimes a person will finish sentences for another. This works when the two are on the same wavelength, but it often isn't accurate. I had someone do that to me repeatedly years ago and it frustrated me. I finally said something bizarre and random at the end of a sentence, just to see what would happen and it was rather amusing to me and confusing to her! This person assumed she knew what I was going to say; therefore, she was not really listening to me.

The good news is that active listening is something you can improve on very quickly if you are willing to try. Test this out on an unsuspecting person and you will find you are doing a better job in a very short amount of time. Of course, to get really good at it will take a lot longer, but even just taking the time to read this list and thinking about what you do will help get you onto the right track.

Ten Ways to Improve Your Active Listening Skills

1. **Are you looking at the person?** Is the TV off and your phone put away so you can concentrate? If you are at work, are you still looking at your computer screen, or can you turn away from that to face the person? Getting rid of anything that will distract you is a good way to get active in your listening. Eye contact—not in a creepy, staring-contest sort of way—is important here.

2. **Can the person tell you are listening?** A big part of being a good listener is helping the other person feel listened to. Are you nodding or smiling appropriately? Are you making small encouraging sounds, like "uh-huh" or "wow" or "I see" to let them know you are hearing them? (You probably do this automatically, and just don't have a name for it.)[15] If you are on the phone, do nothing else and focus on the voice you are listening to. Remember, you are "listening," not talking.

3. **Try using your curiosity** to question anything you don't understand, hear, or believe about what they are saying. It's okay to interrupt someone nicely if you want them to clarify something they said that isn't making sense to you ... as long as you use "I" language

---

[15]As I've already said, the technical name for these words is "minimal encouragers."

to do that. For example, "I'm sorry to interrupt, but I thought I heard you say you didn't want to go. Can you tell me more about that?" Use your own vocabulary, of course; this is just an example.

4. **Use paraphrasing** (repeating back in your own words what you heard the other person say) to be sure that you understand what the person is telling you. This is really helpful if someone at work is asking you to do a number of things and you want to make sure you don't miss anything. For example, a supervisor says to you: "Kelsey, I want you to order some widgets, send an email to everyone to let them know you've ordered them, and maybe find out when they'll be delivered, and include that in the email so that people stop asking me when we're going to get more in." In order to paraphrase that, you might say something like: "Okay, so you want me to call the company and find out how fast they can ship us some widgets, and then let everyone know in an email that I ordered some and when they will probably arrive?" Supervisor: "Exactly. Thanks." Same communication, paraphrased for clarity and accuracy. When you do that, you will be sure you won't miss any of the instructions.

5. **Focus on the other person, not on yourself.** If you are trying to be a better listener, don't latch onto what the other person is saying and launch into a story about yourself. This then stops being a listening exercise and becomes all about you. If you seriously want to be a better listener, wait until the other person has finished their story.

6. **Try not to interrupt** unless you need to clarify

something they just said. I really have to watch this, because I interrupt when I shouldn't, and it's because my brain goes a mile a minute and wants to interject. When this happens to you, resist the urge, and wait.

7. **Use open-ended questions to encourage conversation**. An open-ended question is one that you can't answer with a yes or a no. An open-ended question usually starts with one of the five W's—who, what, where, when, and why—and can also start with how or with something like, "tell me about ... ." These kinds of questions will get more out of the other person than simply asking a yes or no closed question.

8. **Use silence**. We aren't always comfortable with silence in North America, but it's a fabulous tool to get people to open up and talk, especially if they think you are really, actively listening. Sometimes, a well-placed pause will get them talking again, because the natural tendency is to rush in and fill the void.

9. **Listen beyond words**. Watch the other person's body language for clues about how they are doing and what's going on for them. Listen to how they say things—not just to what they say—to their paralanguage. If you get the sense that there is more going on than the words the person is using, get curious and ask them about it in order to communicate better, and more authentically.

10. **Resist problem-solving**. Listening is just that ... listening, not offering to fix things or solve things or to give advice. It amazes me that I will often ask people what listening means to them, and after some usual answers, they offer that they are really good listeners because they always give good advice to their friends

and relatives. It seems that advice-giving is somehow connected with listening for these people. However, I would like to suggest listening and advice-giving are different topics. Just because we humans seem to think we know exactly how everyone else should live their lives, doesn't mean we a) are right about it, or b) have the right to tell them. If someone asks you to help solve their problems or asks for advice, that's one thing; but assuming that's what they want is a dangerous path to choose in communication, and definitely is not part of actively listening.

3. Ask Good Questions

I mentioned the importance of curiosity a while back, and it's important to remember that when what the other person is saying doesn't make any sense to you or doesn't sit well or somehow seems insulting or wrong. Staying emotionally neutral (yes, this is not easy for some of us), thinking before you speak, and then asking with curiosity if the person can explain what they meant when they said what they said, will take you miles.[16] Chances are you didn't hear them correctly or didn't interpret their paralanguage or body language correctly. This can happen and it does happen, a lot. So being able to use curiosity is a very useful skill.

If you want a yes or a no answer, try asking a closed question. This is one that has absolutely only one answer. For example,

"Would you like me to have the report to you Wednesday morning?"

---

[16]Or kilometres if you are in Canada or the UK

"Yes, I would."

or,

"Would you like chocolate ice cream for dessert?"

The answer can **only** be "yes!"[17]

Closed questions are really useful when you need a quick and definite response, such as in an emergency situation when you want to know the ambulance is on its way, or when asking the control tower if you can land your plane, or when responding to a marriage proposal. You definitely just want to hear a one-word answer in these cases.

If you want a longer answer, or if you want to chat to someone and keep them talking, then try using an open-ended question. As discussed earlier, these situations allow you to practise your active listening skills while the other person is talking. Open-ended questions require the other person to say more than just yes or no, and so are excellent for getting to know someone. For example,

"Hi *co-worker's name*, how did you come to be working at this company?"

This is a far more useful question than asking if your co-worker has worked there for long, because he or she could simply say yes, or could just name the number of years he or she has been working there. You'll get a longer and likely a more interesting response with an open-ended question.

Practise asking random people in your life open-ended questions for a week and see how good you get at it. This is good practice and you might end up having some great conversations!

---

[17]Okay, okay, for those of you who are lactose intolerant, there could be another answer.

WHAT DO YOU SOUND LIKE? LET'S TALK VOCAL TONE

As I write this, I'm sitting in a very-well-known coffee chain, working away with my large "for-here" mug of java with a shot of vanilla, listening to the girl behind the counter call out to a customer that his drink is ready. Her voice is sugary-sweet, sing-song, and high-pitched, and full of impossibly adorable cheer. Later, when no customers are at the counter, she is chatting with her co-workers in a totally normal-sounding (still high-pitched, mind you, but that's how her voice is) vocal tone, without all the embellishment.

Interesting.

We sometimes switch into unusual voices depending on our circumstances. Have you heard people speak to babies? Sometimes, they get all gooey and silly, and it's no wonder that babies smile back! Or what about when people talk to their pets? All sorts of strange voice variations come out when people encounter a tiny little puppy. Often, the voice gets higher-pitched and often begins with a loud "AWWWWW!" sound followed by some funny yet unintelligible blathering. Then, when they meet a big, burly, and beautiful Great Dane, their voice may get gruff and deep as they say such things as, "Well, hello, big mister! Aren't you a handsome fellow?"

We are strange creatures.

What do you do around babies and pets?

DO *YOU* HAVE A "WORK" VOICE?

Many people have a particular "voice" they put on only when at work. Ask anyone who has worked for a major hotel or restaurant to talk the way they answer the phone at work, and they will put on their "hotel" voice for you. The movie guy at the start of all those movies, the deep, rich voice that narrates such beginnings as, "In a world where there are few options ..." is a great example.

You know what I mean. Even my own podcast intro man doesn't sound the way he sounds on my show when he's goofing around with the puppy.

Being aware of vocal tone can help you sound professional. It is one thing to say the right words, and another to say them in a tone that is pleasant, confident, and helpful. If you ask the client how you can help them and your tone conveys disinterest, the message you will be sending will not be genuine. If you match your words with your tone of voice, you will be sending a very clear message that you would sincerely like to help.

Genuine or Fake: How You Come Across

It is possible to change how you come across by paying more attention to how genuine your voice sounds. If you are putting on the work voice[19] (which many of us do because it works), are you actually interested when you say things like, "How is your day going?" to a co-worker while lined up at the microwave? Are you paying attention to the

---

[19]I got complimented once on my "church voice," a comment I wasn't exactly sure how to respond to, so I asked the person what she meant. She said she liked the way I spoke loudly, slowly, and clearly when leading the worship service. (I'm a minister in the United Church of Canada in a half-time capacity, just in case you didn't catch that part. And, no, I will not be talking religion or try to convert you, I promise.) And that's when I paid attention to my "work voice" and realized, I do speak differently when up in front of that particular crowd than I would in front of a group of students in my classroom. Strange, but true.

details of what they are saying, or are you wondering how long the whole microwave thing is going to take because you want to go sit outside? Does your vocal tone convey genuine interest?

You are your best teacher ... IF you want to be.

Notice whether or not you are actually looking at the person you are talking to, or are you looking past them, or down at your phone, or at the food in your hand, or at your undone shoe laces?[20]

A fast way to not make new friends and to appear to be shallow on the job is to be non-genuine in your small-talk. People are far smarter than you might give them credit, and will figure you out fast if you don't mean what you say. Here's something to keep in mind: Mean what you say, and say what you mean.

Sounds simple, but it takes a whole lot more work than you might think.

ARE YOU A SPEECH DEMON?

The fact that we can change our voices to suit our situations means that we can train ourselves to sound more appropriate and professional if we put our minds to it. Take a little survey before you begin. Ask a friend or family-member you trust to evaluate the sound quality of your voice.

Are you too soft and quiet in your speech?

Are you shy and afraid to speak up? Do people constantly ask you to talk more loudly, or say things to you like

---

[20]Do people actually have shoelaces anymore or has Velcro® taken over the universe?

"pardon?" or "sorry, can you repeat that?" If yes, take a risk, set yourself a goal, and turn up the volume a notch or two until you notice people saying those things less often. It can be annoying and frustrating to others if you speak too softly, and it can mean you go unheard, which would be sad ... because you have great things to contribute.

Is your voice quality dull and boring?

Do you often hear snoring when you speak to a crowd? Does your voice have cadence to it (modulating between higher and lower pitches), or is it monotonous and always on the same note?[21] If you have to make presentations at work and your trusted friends have suggested you might practise varying your tone of speech, then this would be "case-of-beer" worthy advice. You want to invite interest in what you are saying not only through the words you use, but also through the natural music of your vocal inflections.

Do you speak too quickly?

Are you a "Speech Demon"? Are people having trouble keeping up?[22] Are you being asked to repeat yourself on the telephone at work or by co-workers during the day? Sometimes listening to someone who speaks really quickly can be a challenge and can cause miscommunication.

A woman was told by a speech pathologist that one of her children was having trouble learning to speak, because the child couldn't keep up with how fast she had to listen! The woman made a real effort to slow down her speech when she was with the child, and the little girl was soon chattering away intelligibly.

---

[21]If you notice people nodding off when you speak, this may be a clue that your voice is monotone and you are putting people to sleep.

[22]I suffer from this problem. If I'm in front of a crowd, which happens regularly, I have to consciously slow down my speech in order for others to keep up with my yammering. (What a great word! Yammering! Try using it in your next sentence.)

This honest evaluation will help you figure out what it is you want to practise in order to improve your vocal tone. Like anything else, it takes awareness and intention to increase your skill in this area ... and I *know* you can do it!

Sexy Voice Girl

One of my funniest memories while working in the Emergency Department of a busy community hospital is of "Sexy-Voice Girl" ... or SVG, as I will call her for short. I never met this woman, but every time I heard her voice it was memorable. What was most memorable was watching the reaction of everyone around me.

"Attention ... Doctor Roberts ..."

SVG was a switchboard operator who also was responsible for making all the announcements on the overhead PA system. She announced all sorts of things: cars with headlights on, phone calls for doctors, calls for doctors to get up to the delivery room to catch birthing babies, emergency situations (such as "code blue"), and other important announcements.

What was so unusual about "Sexy-Voice Girl" was the tone of voice she adopted when on the loud-speaker. Imagine if you will, a soft, breathy whisper slowly saying, "Dr. Roberts ... call two-two-two. Dr. Roberts ... call two-two-two, please."

Think Marilyn Monroe and you would have it right.

When her voice came over the speakers, people would stop whatever they were doing and stare up at the ceiling. They would get these incredulous looks on their faces, and there would be plenty of giggling and eye-rolling. People would look at one another and shrug their shoulders or shake their heads.

Some people would deliberately stroll past the switchboard department window to see if they could catch a glimpse of the person behind the voice.

While it was funny for the rest of us, I imagine SVG would have been embarrassed to learn what effect she was having on those around her.

VOCAL TIPS AND TRICKS

The good news about your voice is that it is an instrument and, like any other kind of instrument, can be played in a multitude of different ways with some practice. Here are some ways in which you can improve how your instrument sounds. Choose one tip at a time and work on it until you master it and then move on to the next.

- Modulate your voice. Speak at a medium volume so that you can be heard, but aren't shouting.
- Avoid using slang words or casual greetings in a professional setting. Use "hello" and "thank you" rather than "hi" or "thanks." (We'll talk more about this later.)
- Smile before you start, especially if you are on the telephone. Your smile will translate into your tone of voice and you will sound friendlier and might even feel friendlier. Sounds weird, but it works.

- Record yourself. I know, it's painful to listen to your own voice, but it will teach you a tremendous amount about how you speak and how you sound. Read a book out loud or mimic an announcement, and just see for yourself what you sound like.
- Don't end every sentence with a question mark. It makes you sound unsure of what you are talking about and can be really distracting for the listener.
- Learn from good examples. Listen to people around you, especially in business settings where there has been some voice communication training. People who work with the telephone on a regular basis have developed very professional quality voice skills, and sometimes just listening and doing what they do can be the best way to learn.

Chapter Six

Choose Your Words Wisely

The old saying—"Sticks and stones may breaks my bones, but words will never hurt me."—is utterly untrue. Written and spoken words have a real impact on others. Let's take a look at how the actual words we choose can make a difference to our professional image and to how the people we work with might see us.

Watch That Slang!

Language is continually evolving, and words come in and out of fashion, like the clothes we wear. Things that were absolutely acceptable once upon a time (like my bright teal-blue cosy track suit) become completely wrong and horrifying. Hairstyles are like that. Words can be like that, too. Slang, which is meant to be playful, humorous, or casual often happens with the spoken word, and is not as commonly found in print. Slang is the replacing of regular words with something meant to represent them instead, and often comes out of pop culture.

While using slang is perfectly fine in some settings, it probably is not a wise idea in the professional workplace setting. Slang is not the same thing as jargon, which is the industry-related terminology that only insiders would understand. The medical world I spent years in is full of that, and it's completely acceptable and often expected to use jargon when talking to colleagues.

So, saying, "Yo, 'Sup?" instead of "Hello. What's up?" when you answer the phone might be okay when speaking with your buddy, but is not appropriate at work.

Sometimes, words that we think might be in common usage for everyone are actually a form of slang and not business or workplace material quite yet. Take, for example, the new spelling of things. It's pretty rare to see "We'll See You Soon!" on a sign anymore. Instead, you are more likely to see, "We'll C U Soon!" Not really earth-shattering or anything, but my point is that the vernacular (slang, local sayings, etc.) does sneak in eventually. In a casual chat with a co-worker, this is not an issue. In a transaction with a client or during a meeting or presentation, this is not the best way to get your great ideas across, because these things tend to be what people remember. And *definitely* don't use slang in any business email, because unprofessional correspondence may come back to haunt you.

Similarly to slang, texting-words (LOL, for example) and emoticons (cute smiley faces) are also inappropriate to use in professional correspondence, emails, presentations, and report writing. While for many, these additions have become second nature in social media, texting, and personal communication, using them at work will certainly detract from your professionalism.

"Them" Old-Time Clichés and Colloquialisms

Clichés

What is a cliché? Well, it's an old tired saying that (wait for it ... here comes one) "everyone and their dog" says about something, and that you've no doubt heard a thousand times.

Clichés are trite, overused, and often culturally specific words or phrases. People from different cultures may not understand the meaning of clichés. Clichés are also vague in meaning and indicate a lack of creativity in the user, particularly if they are used in written form. There are two forms of clichés: the tired metaphor and common phrases.

Some common clichés:

better late than never
don't judge a book by its cover
we're on the same page
thinking outside the box
if it ain't broke, don't fix it
cool as a cucumber
never say never
it's a game-changer
it's a win-win situation
it's not written in stone
only time will tell
... shall I stop?

You get the idea. I am certainly not immune. I use clichés, and you do too, probably. In fact, I'd be surprised to find someone who didn't ever use a cliché, but it's when and how you use them, where and in what company that counts. Sometimes they just sound condescending. Sometimes, you'll sound like your parent or grandparent ... which is okay if they are cool people ... but *you know what I mean.*

I would suggest dreaming up something unique and

novel to say instead, or maybe (now here's is a new-fangled idea that'll rock your world), say nothing at all!

COLLOQUIALISMS

Like clichés, these are phrases and sayings that are usually spoken rather than written down, and are often regional in nature. For this reason, someone learning English, for example, may have no idea what you are talking about if you tell them it's "raining cats and dogs". (In fact, that could be a little frightening!) Another example: "hiring you for this job was a no-brainer." Colloquialisms work in casual non-workplace settings, and not so well when you want to sound professional.

JARGON

Jargon is language specific to a profession, industry, trade, or sometimes to a brand. (If you've ever ordered a coffee at Starbucks, you will know what I mean.) Jargon is useful and helpful if you are speaking with someone else who is part of the same group you are, because it can save time and be very efficient. It becomes a problem when you are speaking to people outside your industry and you use it, because chances are, you will be speaking a foreign language. Using jargon when speaking to a "lay person" could frustrate, annoy, exclude, or confuse them, and could cause your message to be miscommunicated. It's always best to use proper words and phrases when in doubt, and to reserve your use of jargon for those whom you are sure will understand it.

Filler Words and Fluff

An economy of words is a beautiful thing.

Sometimes, we have pet phrases and little words that we use that we don't even notice anymore, until someone makes us aware of them.

I saw a newspaper article once about a now infamous young performer. It was a word-for-word transcript of a short interview the reporter had conducted with her. I don't have a copy of it anymore and don't recall the exact content, but here is my reimagining of it.

It went something like this:

Reporter: So what is your next project, *(name of star)*?

Star: Well, like, I'm not really [pause] like sure, because I've been on tour for [pause] like ever, and um, I really need some time to [pause] like relax, [pause] like you know what I mean?

Reporter: Sure, I do. Where do you generally like to relax?

Star: (laughs) Oh, like anywhere. Mostly I like those [pause] um ... like all-inclusives that have [pause] like all the food and like you don't have to do [pause] like anything, you know? That's how I like to relax. It's like really important when you work as hard as I do to [pause] like cut yourself a break and [pause] like chill.

Whatever the interview was actually about, it went on for quite a while and it was truly embarrassing to even read. I cut it out, pinned it on my fridge, and made gleeful reference to it to the youngest members of our family, who said the word "like" a lot. I was subjected to a lot of eye-rolling for that move, but they got my point.

Do you have "filler words" that mean nothing, but that you pop into your sentences just because?

I do. I discovered that I say "ummm" a lot, because I have to listen to the podcasts I do during the editing process. I hadn't noticed this before and now I pay much more attention to how I speak "on air."

Some common filler phrases to avoid include these:

- you gotta understand
- actually
- sooooo
- listen
- as you can imagine
- really?
- like
- well
- seriously
- I mean
- you know?
- ya know?
- I gotta tell you
- as you can see
- needless to say
- I guess
- literally
- interesting

Why should you be aware of the filler words you use and limit their use?

Sometimes, they come out most when we're nervous. Filler words can make an otherwise-normal sentence sound messy and long-winded, and can make the speaker sound lacking in confidence, incompetent, or confused. Presentations can take twice as long to finish if they're peppered with filler words and phrases. The audience might wonder if the person really knows what they are doing, because filler words and phrases can give a loud and clear message of inexperience. Some of the words sound weak, or are simply used as padding and mean nothing. At all. These filler words can sometimes end up in our written communication too.

And filler words can annoy people. Which isn't good when you are trying to impress them with your professionalism.

Here is an example of how filler words might pad a sentence:

A manager asks an employee a question about finances during a presentation at a meeting. She catches the employee off-guard. The employee looks for the information and says, "Ummm, sure ... right ... let me just see here ... seriously, you gotta understand I just put this stuff together this morning, so like um ... so ya ... here it is. If you actually look at the actual figures, you'll see that um, we are actually kinda doing okay."

Now see what happens if you strip away all the filler stuff from the very same sentence:

"Sure. I just put this stuff together this morning. Here it is. If you look at the actual figures, you'll see that we are doing okay."

Which one of these responses would have you trusting that the employee knows what he's doing?

The problem with filler words and pet phrases is that we usually don't even know we are saying them, that is, until we hear our voices recorded, or until someone else points them out to us, which is usually hard to hear. Filler words and weak, wimpy, and waffling phrases give a message to others that you are not confident, capable, or competent. This might be absolutely untrue, but that doesn't matter, does it? Perception is powerful. (I keep saying this, I know. Because it's true.)

My suggestion, if you want to eliminate extra, unnecessary words in your speech, is to record yourself speaking and to notice every time you use filler words or pet phrases or "wimpy waffling words," and choose one of these items to work on eliminating. Then move on to eliminate the next one. If you tackle one thing at a time, eventually the words will, "like," be gone, and you will sound like the intelligent and articulate individual you actually are.

Chapter Seven

Work Ethic

Work ethic used to mean the harder you worked and the more you produced, the better. Working harder and faster was seen as having a good work ethic when referring to working in production-type factory jobs, but now working smarter and more efficiently (which might mean you produce less but what you do produce is of higher quality) can be far more valuable.

The term "work ethic" can mean all sorts of things, but mostly it means the way in which you approach your job.

Here are some work ethic questions to think about:

- Do you actively look for opportunities to learn and to figure things out on your own?
- Do you set goals and try to reach them each day so that you learn, improve, and grow?
- Do you work hard and complete tasks assigned to you each day?
- Do you get to work on time, stay until the end of the day, and take appropriate breaks?
- Do you call in if you are going to be late, sick, or absent?
- Do you try to be helpful and supportive to others around you?
- Are you honest, accountable, trustworthy, and reliable?

- Do you take pride in your work and do the best job you possibly can?

If you can honestly answer "yes" to many or most of these questions, then you will be viewed by others as having a great work ethic. If you struggle to answer "yes" to any of them, don't worry, there are things you can do to improve.

You can easily choose one or two of these points and set a goal to do things differently. No one will know what you are consciously trying to do, but what will be interesting to notice is whether or not what you are doing gets noticed.

There is no time like now to start changing the world, and changing how you manage yourself is the very first step.[23]

Time Management: Tips and Advice

Let's look at what time management is, why it's important to master, and ways in which you can increase your skills at it. Time management (or how you organize the things you have to do in the time you have to do them in) is something people are watching you for.

Everything you do—especially in the first three months while on probation in a new job—is going to set the standard for what others can expect from you. How you manage your time is not an exception. If you want to stand out and shine, then you want to work in such a way that

---

[23]I want you to know that you have the power to change how you are viewed for the better and, sometimes, it starts with one single small step. For example, if you are always just a little bit late for work each day, start there. Set the alarm for ten minutes earlier and make it your goal for the next three weeks to get to work even five minutes early. Not earth-shattering, but a first step that is easily achieved.

you imagine yourself being watched and evaluated all the time, even if you aren't actually. This way, you can work on things you want to improve, play by the rules, and really learn the job well.

How you manage time is a form of nonverbal communication. There is even a term for it: chronemics. Your ability to perform your role hinges not only on your training and experience, but also upon your ability to complete the assigned tasks in the allotted amount of time, with efficiency and professionalism. If you are consistently running out of time, your manager is going to notice and will need to find out whether the issue is that the workload is too heavy or that you need to speed up. At the beginning of a new job, you will almost certainly be slower than someone who has been there for a year. Your ability to manage your time effectively in a new job will take several weeks for you to learn, and for the most part, your co-workers and manager will understand this. There are, however, some practices you can engage in right from the start that will make it easier for you to build your time-management capacity.

PUNCTUALITY

It can say a lot about you.

If you are always a few minutes early to work so that you can put away your coat and bags, pop your lunch into the refrigerator,[24] and fire up your computer or get into your overalls, you will be starting to work for your pay right at your official start time.

---

[24]Because of *COURSE* you are eating healthy food and bringing your own bagged lunch to work.

Very professional.

If, however, you wander in ten minutes after your work day is scheduled to start, and *then* start to put your things away, then stop by the coffee pot or the water cooler for a coffee and a chat, you will not be productive until a good twenty-five to thirty minutes into your day.

Not professional at all.

Punctuality is both noticed and expected in someone wanting to shine in the workplace. Being consistently late will make you stand out, not in a good way, and it very clearly communicates that you don't care (even if you actually do) and this will eventually create problems.

Leaving early on a regular basis is just as bad. So is the habit of "leaving before you leave," meaning you start to pack up your desk, shut off your computer, get out of your work gear, retrieve your coat, wander over to the lunchroom to rinse out your coffee mug, and collect your reusable lunch kit about twenty minutes before you are officially off shift. What you communicate by doing this is that you are in a big hurry to leave. This may be true, but if you want to behave professionally, this is not going to help you with that goal.

"Leaving before leaving" **will** be noticed. It means you are disengaged in the work you are being paid to do. Getting ready to leave a few moments before the end of your shift is acceptable (emphasis on the word *few*), but starting the whole leaving process while still firmly "on the clock" is not going to be looked upon favourably.

PRIORITIZING

This is one of those words that shows up in evaluation forms, in interview questions, and in many employee training programs. This should tell you that it's something to pay attention to. Prioritizing is a way of helping you organize yourself and the tasks that you are expected to accomplish in any given work day.

Depending on what kind of workplace you have, your task list might be self-evident, although I would still suggest that there will be things you need to sort into order of importance, no matter what job you are doing.[25]

There are all sorts of tools available to help you prioritize your tasks, and some are better than others. I prefer the old-fashioned list with pen and paper. Some people prefer a big white board or a computerized list.

There are all sorts of downloadable programs and applications available to help with this too. I would mention names, but chances are these will be outdated by the time you read this, so I won't. Look up "time management apps" and you will find dozens. I like these also because they beep and buzz when your time is up and you are supposed to move on to your next task. (At home, I even program in naps, because it's fun to say, "Oh look! I have to stop washing dishes now and take a nap. My app says so.")

Choose whatever helps you to keep organized and that works for you.

---

[25] The aforementioned sandwich-making lady would be wise to make sure the lettuce was washed and cut up for the sandwich station *before* the lunch rush, so that she could have it for the sandwiches. The lettuce would be more important on the priority list than ordering the supplies for the next week, which could be done after the lunch rush was over. You get the idea. Plus, I really wanted to use that big word: aforementioned.

At work, take five minutes at the start of your shift and write down all the tasks, responsibilities, and goals you have for your day, and you will save time and stay on track. You can even assign a timeframe to each task, building in extra time in case you get interrupted, which would alter your timeline. Prioritizing is also about flexibility—the ability to adjust your priorities as things arise is just as important as sorting out your list to begin with.

The point is, having some kind of plan for your workday can be an extremely simple and effective way to improve productivity, to keep you organized, to give you a sense of accomplishment (I love to look back at my list all checked off at the end of the day. It makes me feel like I actually did something), and will cause you to appear to be professional in your approach to your daily duties. Which you will be.

TAKING BREAKS

There are all sorts of other reasons why you should take your breaks.

In some locations, labour law dictates how many breaks a person is to have in a work shift and how long the breaks are to be. If you are working in a unionized environment, then it is expected that you take breaks according to union regulations and the collective agreement.

Dr. James A. Levine is a professor at the Mayo Clinic, and a world-renowned leader in obesity research. He has done studies and written a number of articles examining how taking short physical breaks (even walking on treadmills while standing at desks) can be beneficial to the health of employees. His findings show that workers who remain sedentary without taking breaks throughout the day are impairing their health. He says, "the design of the human being is to be a mobile entity," and even encourages nap breaks if the workplace allows it.[26] Therefore, leaving the workspace entirely for even a short while is good for you, can give your brain a break, which can lead to brilliant new ideas, a fresh perspective, and the ability to come back to a task or problem you have been working on with renewed determination. Really. It "reboots" you.

So it's lunch time. You've been working hard all morning, and it's time to stop for a bit and fill the tummy and relax a bit.

You may not *think* anyone is paying attention to how long you are gone on a break, but chances are they are, especially if they are waiting for you to return so they can take their turn.

Being mindful of how what you do affects your co-workers is part of being a good team member.

If your break is supposed to be thirty minutes, stick to thirty minutes. Those employees who don't and who regularly take extra time, could be answering to the manager during their annual employee performance reviews, and might regret their actions when it's promotion time, or when changing jobs and asking for job references.

People pay attention to these things, sometimes very quietly.

"So what?" you might think. "Nobody cares. Everybody else does it."

---

[26]Korkki, Phyllis. *To Stay on Schedule. Take a Break.* The New York Times. June 16, 2012. www.nytimes.com/2012/06/17/jobs/take-breaks-regularly-to-stay-on-schedule-workstation.html?_r=0 [accessed December 2014]

You may not think anybody cares, and that might be true, but being professional includes paying attention to how you use your time, and is more about self-monitoring than trying to "get away" with something. When you respect the time designated for your coffee and lunch breaks, you are doing the following:

- You are recognizing that you are being paid to work, and that breaks are built in for your benefit.
- You are paying attention and being accountable.
- You are responsible and can be trusted.
- You are practising good time management.
- You want to work.
- Not taking any breaks also speaks volumes.

While you may think you are being more efficient and productive, not taking breaks can send the message that you can't handle the workload or manage your time, that you are inefficient or that you waste time, or that you aren't responsible or trustworthy. While none of these things might be true, perception is powerful, and what people perceive, they believe.

CLIQUES

You are on probation at the start of a new job both officially and unofficially until everyone, including you, figures out where you fit in. How you behave in this time as part of the team will be noticed.

One thing that you as a new employee might wonder about is how you will fit in to the group that existed before you arrived? A good tip to begin with is to watch and pay attention to the dynamics of the team you have joined. Watch and pay attention to the "societies within" or the sub-groups that already exist in your workplace. If you can refrain from rushing in—like an eager puppy wanting his dinner—to join any one particular group, then you will be wiser for it.

Here's what to watch for:

- Who is part of the "in" crowd and who isn't?
- Who would you like to align yourself with?
- What factions are there?
- What cliques are there?

Having this information can help you align yourself with people who are going to be helpful to you in your new situation. It may be best to just observe for a while and to take mental notes and to stay open to everyone at first until you understand how things work.

Every workplace has groups within it, and it can take time to learn who and what they are all about. These might be simply groups of people who have been there the longest who are close to one another and have a shared history. It might be a group of people who love to go out and socialize together outside the workplace. Some of them might be part of an office baseball team. It might be that there are people who have kids and people who don't, or people who are married and people who aren't. Sometimes the divisions and groupings form along generational lines, gender lines, or even role divisions.

Keep in mind that whenever a new employee joins a workplace, the dynamic of the whole changes. Change can be just fine for some people (those who are flexible and resilient), and change can be challenging for others who prefer to resist it. Regardless, your joining the team changes the team dynamic, and my suggestion is that you go in gently and with patience and sensitivity until you find your particular niche.

Gab and Gossip

A sure-fire way to kill any sense of professionalism anyone might have of you in one "swell-foop," as my mother would say, is to participate in office gossip.

Gossip is the discussion of the private and personal details of another person's life, without their consent and in their absence.

Socializing and catching up on what others are up to is appropriate in small doses, and will build community in the workplace, which is a *good* thing and what you want to be doing. Talking about other co-workers in their absence, however, is the fastest way of being disrespected yourself and of having your work buddies wondering whether or not they should trust you.

There is a question I used to ask my children when they were little and totally into the "tattle-tale" phase and it goes like this: **Are you telling me this to be helpful or hurtful?**

This is a useful question to ask yourself if you find you want to tell someone something about another person in your workplace. Force yourself to pause briefly and ask yourself the above question *before* telling your tale; then you will be able to refrain from ruining both your own professional aura, and possibly that of another's.

Gossip is rarely helpful and almost always hurtful.

Malicious gossip—the stuff of soap operas and TV dramas—is pretty much never a smart idea. It's just mean. It's an ugly way to feed your own ego, and to make yourself feel better, which it might well do, but it will be short-lived. If you are the kind of person who takes great delight in talking about the inadequacies or miseries of another human being, ask yourself why.

And get some professional help. (I'm not joking here.)

Here's a story to illustrate how easy it can be to find yourself in such a situation, and how horrible the consequences can be:

A student I was supervising was doing her practicum at the hospital. She was sitting in a booth in the noisy cafeteria with a number of nurses and other staff from the nursing unit she was assigned to. The student had been working there for about three weeks, and was feeling comfortable with the group of co-workers, who seemed to be accepting her as one of the team. The staff began to gossip about the unit manager. Unbeknownst to the entire table, the manager in question was seated in the next booth.

The student, wanting to feel like part of the group and to fit in, joined in and made a negative comment about the manager that got a big laugh. As soon as the laughter subsided, the manager, who couldn't take it anymore, stood up, revealing to the booth next to her that she had been there the whole time. Needless to say, the conversation stopped abruptly and there were more than a few red faces around the table. The manager didn't say anything, but she didn't have to. Lunch was over.

I can only guess what damage had been done in the space of one lunch break.

It was shortly afterward that I was called to a meeting

103

with said manager to deal with the mess. That student was removed from the unit for the rest of the shift, and the consequences were severe. In the end, I think she had the hard and unenviable task of explaining herself to the manager, apologizing, and asking for forgiveness. The damage, however, had been done. I doubt she'd ever get work in that particular hospital.

In a new workplace situation, it is natural to want to fit in, to want people to like you, and to want to feel part of the team. It is also wise to take care to not find yourself in an awkward situation involving gossip from which you cannot extricate yourself.

So, What Can You Do About Office Gossip?

If you feel that a piece of gossip is about to come from your own mouth, ask yourself, "Is what I'm about to say helpful or hurtful?"

Say something nice about the person who is the subject of the gossip. People will soon get the message.

If you find yourself in a gossip-filled conversation, excuse yourself and get busy doing something else. In other words, get out of the zone and refuse to take part.

Or, make a point and simply state (don't judge the gossipers, just make it your own policy) that you don't like to talk about others when they aren't around.

If you don't want to leave, and are assertive enough to pull it off in a way that seems natural, introduce a new topic, and change the direction of the conversation to something more positive.

Gossip is never appropriate. If you are consistent with

your response to it, three things might happen: people will get the message you are not going to play the gossip game, you will be seen to be more professional for that, and you won't get caught in potentially awkward conversations.

P.S. Shouldn't you be working, anyway?

Chapter Eight

Accountability and Learning From Mistakes

Be Accountable for Your Actions

Accountability is a desired quality in an employee, and is even more important in some cases than accuracy. Of course, you want to be accurate in your work and to be efficient and competent, and chances are you will be. At first, however, you will be learning, and in any learning situation there is a fair bit of room for error. When an error is made, it might feel natural to want to find reasons for it and to justify it by blaming circumstances, technology, or other people. This is not a best practice, and not a good idea. It is actually best to, as Shakespeare would say in *Macbeth*, "screw your courage to the sticking place," and admit the mistake. Of course, this can be hard to do for some, and quite easy for others depending on what you are used to doing.

Accountability is definitely a professional quality.

When you are accountable for your actions, when you admit a mistake and ask how best you can fix it, you gain much. You are seen to be honest, you gain respect, you earn trust, and you will have people willing to help you right away to fix the problem, and to help you learn how to improve the next time. Being accountable takes courage and strength, is often unpleasant, and is *always* the best course of action.

A young man I know works as an airplane mechanic. He was busy doing some work on a plane in a hanger, and was driving a wheeled lift past the plane to get to the end of it, when he realized too late that he was too close to the plane and the side of the lift crunched into the plane's door, seriously damaging it. He told me that the only thing he could do that would allow him both peace of mind and to maintain his professionalism was to go directly to his manager and tell him what had happened. No one was happy about the incident, of course, least of all the mechanic. He said that his boss thanked him for being accountable, and said that the young man was worth far more to him as an employee *because* he was willing to be accountable than someone who perhaps was more technically capable or experienced but unwilling to take responsibility for incidents such as this one.

Being accountable is key to being a highly valuable employee in your company.

My Massive Mistake Story

I once made a really big mistake at work. (Okay, I made a few big mistakes at work, but this one is the best story to illustrate my point.)

I was working in a small hospital as a Health Unit Coordinator (Nursing Unit Clerk). A doctor had written an order for me to book an ambulance to send a patient for a specialized test at another hospital in a city thirty minutes away, a fairly common occurrence.

So, I made an assumption.[27] I booked the ambulance, got all the paperwork together, and the next day, the ambulance crew arrived to pick up said patient.

Off they went with the man in his gown all tucked in nicely and strapped down to the stretcher. All was well (or so I thought), until I got a phone call about thirty minutes later from one of the crew members. It turns out the hospital I had sent them to had no idea this patient was coming, had never heard of him, and wasn't going to deal with it. Something had gone terribly wrong with my planning.

I stayed calm, tried to breathe, and told the crew to hang tight while I made a call to the only other hospital in the area that did this test, when I found that, yes, they were expecting the very patient to arrive on their doorstep any moment to begin his procedure.

The first time I took responsibility for the mistake was right then, when I explained my initial assumption to the clerk on the phone who was expecting the missing patient, apologized, and asked what, if anything, could be done to ensure the procedure could still take place that day. After sighing heavily, she put me on hold. Eventually she said they could rearrange things to make it work. Luckily for me, they were able (and willing) to be flexible.

---

[27]Never a good idea.

The ambulance crew, however, wasn't so sure. I explained my mistake, apologized, and again asked what could be done. After a quick call to dispatch and more flexibility, the patient got to where he was supposed to be and had the test.

The third time I had to explain what was going on was to the Charge Nurse, and luckily I was able to tell her things had been organized and the test was still going to proceed.

I was deeply relieved because there had been patient preparation for the procedure, both physically and emotionally, and if things had not gone as they eventually did, I would have been answering to the doctor who had ordered the test, to the nurses who had prepped the patient, to the patient himself, and possibly also to his family. Rebooking and reordering would then be required, which, in our Canadian system, could mean weeks of waiting, and there would have been the monetary cost to the system of transporting a patient via ambulance for nothing, not to mention the potential compromise to the patient's health as a result of my mistake.

The whole thing was embarrassing, and a good lesson both in the consequences of assumption and in admitting a mistake immediately and doing everything in my power to fix it.

What to Do if You Mess Up

And so, it is crucial that you practise accountability. We all make mistakes, and owning up to them earns you much more respect than if you try to assign blame or make excuses.

It is also best to own up to a mistake as soon as you possibly can, so that you can figure out how to fix it and move on. I have found that both in the workplace and in non-work relationships, saying, "I made a mistake. I'm sorry. How can I fix this?" is the absolute best way to get back on track.

It isn't easy, though. Saving face is something we all try to do instinctively, which is why it can feel easier to blame others or make excuses ... because it hurts the ego and bruises the pride to be wrong.

But it isn't easier in the end. The fastest way to get on with things is to admit to making the mistake. Own it. It will be uncomfortable for a bit or maybe longer, depending on how serious the mistake is, but the key thing is to be accountable, be honest, be apologetic, and then figure out what the next step is to fix the situation.

Here's the thing: you are going to make mistakes. And mistakes are excellent ways to learn really important lessons.

- You will stand out and shine if you believe that being honest with others begins with being honest with yourself first.
- You will stand out and shine if you are willing to admit to not being perfect.
- You will stand out and shine if you are accountable for your actions.

LEARNING FROM YOUR MISTAKES

Mistakes are actually fabulous opportunities. While it might feel like you've failed at first, a mistake is a perfect window into how to do things better, which is ultimately what you want to do as a new employee. It's not about being the corporate automaton: fitting into the box, not making waves, and doing what you're told. No, because anyone can do that. What you want to do is stand out, not as in being better than anyone else, but as in being the best "you" you can possibly be. That means being creative and innovative, being kind, being generous with your knowledge and your time, being insightful, being able to anticipate the needs of those around you, and being willing to grow and learn.

What Silly Putty®, the Slinky®, Chocolate Chip Cookies and Scotchgard™ Have in Common

Mistakes are often how incredible innovations happen.[28] Here are four examples of innovations that were each the result of a simple mistake.

Silly Putty® was never supposed to have happened. An engineer at General Electric named James Wright was trying to make an alternative to rubber. Rubber was in short supply during World War II, because of attacks on countries that grew and produced it. The US Government decided to find an alternative. During a test that Wright was doing with silicon oil, he added boric acid to the mix, which ended up being a mess of goo that did weird things like stretch beyond how rubber stretched, didn't grow mould, and even bounced when dropped! While it was a very strange and fun substance, it wasn't going to

---

[28]Alyson Krueger, "15 Life-Changing Inventions That Were Created By Mistake." Businessinsider.com. November 16, 2010. businessinsider.com/these-10-inventions-were-made-by-mistake-2010-11?op=1 [accessed December 15, 2014]

work for the war effort. Wright carried on working, and the substance eventually ended up being shared, the recipe sold, and eventually in the1950s, put into plastic eggs, and turned into a toy that kids still love today. And all from a mistake.

The Slinky® was another oops! In 1943 a naval engineer named Richard Jones was working with tension springs. He accidentally dropped one on the floor and it kept bouncing. He watched it for a bit and got a great idea, and went home to tell his wife, who named it. In 1946, the toy was a hit at the American Toy Fair, and is still being sold today using the original design.

Chocolate chip cookies were invented by accident. In the 1920s, Ruth Wakefield and her husband owned a bed-and-breakfast-type establishment called the Tollhouse Inn. Ruth did the cooking, and one of her most popular offerings was her cookies. Her usual recipe called for baker's chocolate that melted into the butter-filled cookies. One day she discovered she was out of baker's chocolate, so instead she chopped up a bar of semi-sweet chocolate that had been gifted to her by a guest named Andrew Nestlé, an owner of the Nestlé chocolate company. Instead of melting away like the baker's chocolate usually did, the bits stayed whole and the rest is delicious history.

Scotchgard™ is the result of yet another useful mistake, although the environmental safety of some of the ingredients is now under question. Patsy Sherman, a chemist, was working for the 3M Company in the 1950s developing a synthetic rubber to use in the fuel lines of airplanes ... something that wouldn't erode or break down when coming into contact with jet fuel. She had made a batch of synthetic latex, which was in a glass bottle. A lab assistant accidentally dropped the glass bottle, which broke, splashing some of the contents on her shoe. It wouldn't come off no matter what they did, and after a period of time they noticed that the spot where the shoe had been splashed was clean and wasn't getting dirty, even when the rest of the shoe was. Eventually Sherman took out a patent and sold the substance, which ended up being used to protect carpets and furniture from spills and dirt.

My point?

Sometimes mistakes are the best things that could ever happen.

If nothing incredibly brilliant and lucrative comes of your mistake, at least see it as the chance to do better the next time, and try your best not to repeat the same mistake. Mistakes that don't initially seem to have happy results often produce wisdom that surfaces long after the event. Athletes and artists become much better at what they do through the learning they gain from repeated mistakes. Entrepreneurs can tell you countless stories of failed product attempts before finding what worked. As an employee, you will find places in your new job where you naturally excel, and places where you won't until and once you've made several mistakes and learned from them. If you truly learn from the mistakes you make, you will grow as an employee, and more importantly, as a person.

How to Fail Gracefully and Learn From It

For some people, it's not failing that's the issue, it's the *fear* of failing that terrifies them. This fear sometimes paralyzes people and causes them to want to hide in their rooms and play games on the internet all day, because that is safer and easier than taking a chance, than risking, than possibly failing at something.

Learning to fail gracefully is a bona fide skill and is important to have as a new employee, because there is always more to learn in the workplace.

We aren't given much opportunity to practise the art of failing well. In elementary school, every child gets a ribbon for participating in Sports Day or in the speech competition or the spelling bee. At birthday parties, every guest gets a "goodie bag" full of treats, so that the birthday child isn't the only one getting gifts. Games are created so that everyone is included, and if a grade-school child doesn't actually make the grade, it's rare they are ever held back and have to repeat a year.

While I understand the thinking behind wanting to lessen the competition and wanting everyone to feel included, important, and special, I wonder if this kind of practice doesn't set people up in the future for heartache when they realize that in the grown-up world, there is no ribbon for participation, they aren't particularly special, and there isn't a prize or an award given for everything they do.

If You Are a Human Being, You Will Fail

And failing can actually be good ... in the end.

We fail when we are learning to tie shoelaces when we are tiny, and by trying again, we learn.[29] We fail when we first try to get square blocks into round holes in our toys and eventually we master the game. We fail when we lose a

---

[29]Because of the invention of Velcro, thousands actually have lost this skill and never learn!

video game, don't make it into the school play, or don't get our dream job. There are opportunities to learn all along the way, and these are good moments to realize that the world isn't actually against us in our efforts. If, instead of getting upset, we could sit back, take a breath, and figure out how to try again, we would be wiser the next time.

Most of us learn from experience, and most of us could benefit from learning how to manage failure gracefully and thoughtfully.

A mother I know told me a story of her son coming home with an "F" on his math test. She smiled at him and said to him something like, "That's good. Now what will you do next?" He looked at her with surprise and said, "How can an 'F' be good?"

"It's not that the 'F' is good, son; it's the opportunity to learn from getting the 'F' that's a good thing."

When he still looked confused, she continued, "Did you study as much as you could have?"

He shook his head.

"Did you hand in all your homework assignments for this topic?"

Again, he shook his head.

"When you weren't sure about something, did you go and ask the teacher for extra help?"

"No." He sounded miserable.

"Well, then, you've learned something, haven't you? What are you going to do next time?"

"All that stuff?" he looked up at her.

"Yes ... and my guess is, you won't be bringing home another 'F' if you do."

Life didn't end. He had failed a test. And in the process, he figured out that it didn't feel very good to fail, and that there were steps he could take so that it didn't happen again.

Failing doesn't feel very nice, and the fear around the consequences is actually worse than failing itself:

- What will my manager think of me?
- What will my co-workers say?
- I must not be smart.
- I'm never going to understand this.

You can see how it works. It's therefore easier (or so it might seem) to not even try to advance in the first place. But then if you don't try, you won't ever accomplish anything.

All successful people in life have learned how to fail. All of them.

So how can you learn to fail gracefully?

HAVE A GAME PLAN

Talk to any successful business person about their failures, and they'll give you a list of them! A successful person might look as if everything they touch is successful, but if you dig a little deeper, you'll learn that he or she has stories of failing and of learning from the experience and trying again. Sometimes, this cycle repeated itself multiple times before the success happened, and then of course, nobody remembers the failures.

Most success is built on a foundation of failure.

Or, put another way, successful people have learned many things as they have practised their craft.

Becoming successful in the workplace has to do with persistence, perseverance, and practice. It also has to do with managing what doesn't work well, in order to proceed with your goals.

A plan to help with this involves imagining both the success you want and what might actually happen. Write your plan down. What is it you wish to achieve and how will you do that?

Perhaps you intend to work in a particular department.

Perhaps you want to be given new and more key responsibilities.

Maybe you want to be promoted into a new role.

Ask yourself: If my plan doesn't work, what will happen? And write those answers down.

For example, if I don't get the promotion, where will I be? What will the consequences of not achieving my goal be?

- I will still be doing what I am doing now.
- I will be sad or disappointed.
- I will not take the trip to Mexico I was hoping to take.

Next ask yourself this question: And what will I do next? (This is *key*, because this is how you create an action list.) Write these answers down too.

- If I don't get the promotion, I'll ask the manager why I wasn't chosen.
- I will ask for feedback about my current performance.
- I will work on learning more about what it would take to be promoted.
- I'll ask the manager for regular feedback in the coming months.
- I'll concentrate on doing the best work I can do where I am now.

- I'll seek more training.

The value in doing this exercise is that if you don't succeed in your desired goals immediately, you have an action plan ready to guide you toward succeeding eventually. Spending some time creating this plan will take the fear out of failing and allow you to move gracefully through whatever happens and on to the next step. And along the way, you'll be learning many valuable lessons

FEEDBACK: THE GOOD, THE BAD, AND THE UGLY

What exactly is feedback?

Feedback is information given to an employee about how he or she is performing on the job. It is somewhat like criticism, and is intended to be helpful to the person receiving it.

Workplace feedback sometimes comes in the form of a formal employee performance review once a year, or it can come spontaneously, whenever the boss wants to do one and as often as the need arises. Feedback can be both about how well you as a worker are doing something, or it can be a list of ways you can improve your performance. Feedback can be as simple as a "good job" or pat on the back.

On the job, feedback doesn't just come from management. You can easily give (or get) good feedback to a co-worker (and by "good," I don't mean necessarily praise; good feedback can simply mean effective feedback) and if it's done carefully using your "I" language and some rehearsal first, to supervisors too.

This can be a top-down, bottom-up, or lateral experience.

Feedback is not the same thing as advice. It is also, in a perfect world, based on how you do something, not on who you are as a person. This is really important, because it often gets confused. Telling someone she is really nice is "nice," but isn't very useful as far as feedback goes. Telling the same someone that you appreciate how kind and patient she is when assisting a customer is better feedback. It is more a comment on her action and behaviour than on who she is as a person.

There are some very basic things to think about when giving and receiving feedback.

Receiving feedback

- Try to avoid being defensive. Listening is really important when receiving feedback.
- If you don't agree with something, get curious. Ask lots of questions, and be specific. Again, try not to get defensive.
- Look at feedback as a gift. It is the chance to improve upon what you are doing. It's a way to show that you are "teachable" and can accept constructive criticism and that you can improve.
- You don't have to agree with feedback given. You can thank the person for their comments and be noncommittal. Not all feedback is fair, and, like the upcoming story about a manager and her style of dress, not all feedback is motivated by wanting to be helpful. You might need time to go away and think about what's been offered before you respond. In fact, it might be better to take some time to respond, especially if you don't agree with what was being shared.

Giving and receiving feedback is a very important part of both workplace life and home life too. We can't effectively let people know what's bothering us if we don't speak up, but the way in which we speak up can make the difference between feedback being a useful and effective tool and just a difficult and uncomfortable experience.

GIVING FEEDBACK

The same principles apply to giving feedback in workplace settings and home settings. Something to keep in mind when giving feedback to others is that it can be difficult for the other to receive what you have to say, and so, being sensitive in your delivery is crucial. Here are eight points to consider:

1. Check your motivation. Why are you giving this feedback? Are you telling me to be helpful or hurtful?

> The manager was an eclectic dresser. She was also beautiful and wore clothing that suited her. Her secretary made it her mission each day to make some kind of comment about her boss's clothing, and at first, the manager did think the secretary was trying to be helpful, but after a while, it became really obvious that she was being anything but. The secretary made comments like, "I just don't want anyone to say anything that might hurt your feelings, but you know that your shoes don't actually match that outfit, right?" or "Interesting ... I thought patterned tights were from last year ... you might want to find out, just in case." or "That

121

colour looks good on you, but you might want to wear a little more blush."

Finally, the manager realized that this was not helpful feedback at all, instead it was hurtful. At first, she wasn't sure what to do, but then she decided to be direct. The next morning when the secretary made her usual commentary, the manager stopped her mid-sentence and said very politely, "I'm actually not interested in what you think of my clothing and I'd really appreciate it if you'd stop commenting on it." (Notice the "I" language?) The comments stopped. The secretary's motivation for giving the feedback was not meant to help.

2. Be timely. Give feedback immediately or as soon as possible ... don't let it sit for days or weeks or it will be stale and may even be irrelevant. Feedback is most effective as soon as possible after the event or incident, and then it can be released. It's quite useless to give feedback to someone on something that happened three months earlier. Plus, you don't want it to fester.

3. Be aware of where you happen to be physically when you give feedback. Are you in a private location? Are there people around to hear it? Feedback (especially negative feedback) needs to be given somewhat confidentially and not in front of everyone else in the room.

4. Use "I" language. Talk about what you notice when giving feedback. Don't interpret what you think the other person was thinking, because you really have no idea, unless you happen to be a mind-reader. Also don't rationalize the actions of the other person by making excuses for them. Just be clear and state what you noticed, without attaching anything more to it.

5. Be specific. Saying something like, "You're not nice to me" is unhelpful. Give detailed specific instances the other person can address.

6. Give feedback about things that the other person can actually change. Telling someone their eyes are too small for their face, for example, aside from being just mean and rude, is unhelpful and unchangeable. The whole idea of giving feedback is so that the other person, should they choose to, can make some changes in their behaviour.

7. If you are giving negative feedback, try to give some positive feedback, too. But don't overdo the positive feedback. If you throw too much information at a person, buried in positive feedback, the only thing the person might come away with is the positive, and your negative (or constructive) feedback might get lost.

8. Ask for the person's reaction to what you are saying. They might disagree completely with what you are saying, or be unaware that what they are doing is not good.

A student was coming across as a know-it-all during her clinical experience at the hospital. She would say, "Oh ya, I know; I just forgot." whenever anyone corrected anything she did, and after several incidents of this, people got annoyed and the gossip started. She was labelled as "knowing everything," and people were unimpressed. So unimpressed that they stopped trying to help her at all.

When I heard about what was going on, I took her aside and asked her if she realized how she was coming across to others in the department. She was truly horrified. She had come from working in another hospital area, and was terrified that the people she had worked with would think she didn't know what she was doing in her new role. Her fears were around not proving to her former co-workers that she could do this new job. She had built herself a protective shell, and any feedback or criticism felt like an attack, so she was responding in a way that to her, felt protective, and to everyone else, felt stuck up and know-it-all. Different perspectives.

It is important to check with the person to whom you are giving feedback to find out how your message is being received, Allow them to ask questions to clarify if they need to.

Effective feedback can be a very valuable tool.

Chapter Nine

Managing Stress

What Is Stress?

Stress is a normal response of the body and is actually useful sometimes. Its purpose is actually to keep you safe from danger. Sometimes, it's also useful to keep you alert. Good stress can allow you to do things you don't normally do—it can be the stress of excitement, of new adventures, of taking risks. Good stress can keep you on your toes, keep you from getting lazy, and can ensure you do your very best.

When stress gets to be too much and starts to overwhelm you, well then, it's not good at all; it's dangerous. It can affect everything from your mood, your health, your relationships, and your performance at work.

It can seriously suck the joy out of life. Too much stress is bad.

Stress responses are different in every person. It is really important that you know what your stress signals are so that you can learn how to de-stress when you are tipping over into the danger zone.

Some Common Signs of Stress:

- clenching your teeth or your jaw
- difficulty sleeping
- sleeping too much

- hair loss
- lack of appetite
- memory troubles
- stomach ache
- digestive system problems, such as nausea and diarrhea
- eating too much
- irritability
- inability to focus
- anxiety or worry
- feeling overwhelmed
- withdrawing from usual activity or neglecting responsibilities
- dizziness
- pounding heart
- chest pain
- substance use or overuse
- skin problems, like acne or eczema flare ups
- panic attacks
- depression

Chronic stress can actually lead to serious illness, so it's critical that you know when you are stressed and get ready to do something about it before that happens. Pay attention to what is going on in your body, because your body is brilliant. It knows often before the brain knows when enough is enough. Sometimes, your body will develop a cold or an illness, just to get you to slow down or just stop! If you are stressed, your immune system gets low. If your immune system is low, your body can't heal itself, which it's really good at doing if only we help it.

You aren't going to be able to avoid stress all the time,

of course, because life is stressful for most people at least some of the time. What you can do is lessen stress as much as possible.

Managing Stress at Work

Sometimes, stress in the workplace is part of the job. I've worked in a few jobs over the years that have had stress built in. As a restaurant server in my early days, stress was part of the lunch rush and part of dealing with rude and unreasonable customers. As a Health Unit Coordinator working in the Emergency Department of a busy hospital, stress was an everyday occurrence and expected. As a church minister being called at 3:00 a.m. because a grandmother's tiny grandchild was taken to the Intensive Care Unit and put on life-support and then later died ... stress goes with the territory. As a parent ... well ... just imagine. There are other jobs that have even more stress built into them. Ambulance crews, fire crews, police, air traffic controllers, nurses, doctors, CEOs negotiating multimillion-dollar deals, soldiers, reporters and medics in war zones, ninth grade teachers; the list could go on and on.

We're never going to be able to completely eliminate stress in the workplace, but being able to be in the best possible shape to handle it is critical. Workplace stress inevitably spills over into the rest of your life if not managed well. You don't want ulcers and heart disease. Knowing your stress triggers (things that you already know stress you out) and your own personal stress signals (how your body lets you know you are under stress) will help you to develop strategies to manage *before* you get overwhelmed. Developing awareness and coping strategies early in your work life is a good idea.

One of the bonuses of being able to handle stress well is that it will be noticed by your supervisors, which could lead to added responsibilities and offers of new challenges or opportunities. And the phrase "able to manage stressful situations calmly" looks good on a performance review.

Here are eleven things you can do to manage stress while on the job and off.

Call in Your Support System

That's what friends are for. Talk to someone close to you about what's stressing you and decompress with a good listening ear. If you don't have anyone you can trust with what you need to talk about, find a coach or counsellor who can help you. Sometimes paying someone is a reliable and confidential way to get things off your chest. Starting a new job is stressful, and sharing that with others can help.

Remember to Breathe

When we become stressed, often we breathe very rapidly and shallowly, which is ultimately challenging for our immune system. Taking three deep cleansing breaths whenever you remember will do a lot for your nerves, not to mention your circulation, and will have the overall effect of calming you. And this can be done at work very easily when you feel stressed.

Speak Less, Listen More

If you find yourself in the middle of an intensely stressful situation, try to recognize that, breathe, try to listen more, and speak less. (This will stop you from saying something you'll regret later, and will allow you time to think.) Remember to use "I" language when you do respond. Watch that your body language is not confrontational. Ask for some time to think about what's being said if you need it, and seek advice from higher up the management ladder if you think you need it.

EXERCISE

For many people, going for a run, taking in a yoga class, stretching on the floor, swimming, walking, or working out at the gym are some of the best ways to de-stress. Exercise releases the "happy hormones" (endorphins) into our system and, besides being really good for us physically in multiple ways, is an excellent way to gain perspective and feel better able to handle things. Some workplaces have workout rooms, employee fitness programs, or incentive options at outside fitness facilities.

TAKE A BREAK

If you find yourself in the middle of a stressful situation at work, and feel your body responding to the stress in unhealthy ways, it might be a good idea to pay attention to it and take steps. If you can, get away from the situation for a few minutes and give yourself a chance to take some of those deep breaths, clear your head, and get a little per-spective. Getting right out of your physical work area can help with that. Take your coffee break and go outside, visit a nearby cafe, take a walk, or, if none of these things are possible, take a short breather in the washroom. If your stressor is something that isn't physical, then take what I like to call a brain break, which can be as simple as having a conversation with a co-worker that is non-work related and maybe sharing a laugh. Laughter is a fabulous way to decompress.

EAT CHOCOLATE

Unless, of course, you struggle with food addictions, are allergic or don't like chocolate. Research presented in 2014 at a meeting of the American Chemical Society reported that certain intestinal bacteria consume chocolate (dark cocoa in this case), grow, and ferment it, and then produce anti-inflammatory compounds that are beneficial to the heart and could even reduce the long-term risk of stroke. Dr. John Finley headed the team and noted other overall health benefits of eating chocolate when combined with certain fruits and prebiotics.[30] Not only will eating chocolate release some endorphins in your brain, it is actually good for the rest of you too.

MEDITATE OR PRAY

Many people find that meditation or a practice like centring prayer can refocus them. Such practices have been shown to reduce stress, calm nerves, and allow for an enhanced ability to handle stressful situations. There are several good online resources for learning how to meditate or pray contemplatively, and there are even apps to help with guiding the process.

---

[30]Monte Morin. "Chemists Discover Secret to Dark Chocolate Benefits." *Science Now: Los Angeles Times.* March 18, 2014. latimes.com/science/sciencenow/la-sci-sn-secret-to-dark-chocolates-health-benefits-20140318-story.html [accessed December 15, 2014]

TAKE A BATH

This goes with taking a break; however, that's not usually possible at work. A warm bubble bath once you are home, with candles and music, can help you decompress and relax. A hot-tub is nice too. A hot-tub with a friend is even better. (Wink.)

SNUGGLE YOUR POOCH

Your cat or dog is non-judgmental, in-the-moment, and probably willing to hear all your woes. Animals are known to be stress-reducers, providing of course that they are not the source of your stress in the first place.[31] Some work-places allow employees to bring pets with them, and others have pets as part of the staff! I worked in an extended care unit once that had a resident cat, and the benefits to the staff were just as evident as those to the residents who stopped by several times a day to give Clyde a cuddle.

EAT HEALTHY FOOD

Eat healthy, nourishing food. When your body gets the proper nutrients and the fuel it needs, it functions a whole lot better and is better able to handle the effects of stress. Scarfing down fries and greasy burgers with a shake might make you feel better when you are under stress, but that benefit will last about fifteen minutes. Then you will likely feel awful and guilty, and your body will not be any better

---

[31] I must say that sometimes the puppy causes more stress for us with his chewing on furniture and waking up ridiculously early to go outside, but when he's asleep and cute, or wanting a snuggle, then it's all worthwhile, and snuggling certainly reduces stress.

off for it; neither will your stress level. Some people even find the cooking part of eating healthy to be therapeutic. Watch a cooking show, go find a local farmer's market, take a cooking class. You might find that it's both relaxing and stress-relieving to prepare your own good food (including your lunch for work). Then eating it is, of course, the best!

Get Enough Sleep

This can be a challenge if you are as busy a person as I happen to be, but sleep is essential for keeping everything working well, and most of us in North America are sleep-deprived, which tends to explain the high stress levels and record numbers of people on antidepressants. Good sleep can make you feel a whole lot more like you are able to handle whatever it is that is stressing you out, especially if it is work-related. Lack of sleep also affects your immune system. Working to get a good night's sleep on as regular a basis as possible will help to reduce your overall stress and help you to shine more brightly on the job.

Chapter Ten

Managing Conflict, Being Self-Aware, and Developing Assertiveness

Got Conflict? How to Manage and Reduce It

Not all conflict is bad news. In fact, sometimes conflict is healthy.

Sometimes conflict (which just means a difference of opinion) can bring about great creativity and amazing results that would never have happened otherwise.

Sometimes though, conflict means "a big ol' fight." And it can be downright nasty.

Many people are afraid of conflict ... terrified of it even. We've been told not to show anger, to get along, to share and play well with others and, in some cases, we work really hard at avoiding conflict in order to "play nice."

Sometimes, we even avoid having conversations we know are going to be hard to have. There are all sorts of avoidance games we play with ourselves, and even though we know things need to be said, we don't say them. Or instead we barge into conversations without any preparation or thinking about what might be the best way to approach the topic, which then can end in not-so-nice ways of behaving. Bursting out without thought is not usually a good idea, and is often regretted later.

There are five different conflict management styles that people tend to default to most of the time. This doesn't mean we don't go to any other style on occasion, but in general, we each have a pet-style we like to use. It's a really good idea to know what style is your usual one, so that you can recognize it in the moment (when you are about to execute it), and then maybe try to use one that is more effective.

Again, you can find whole books and blogs on this topic and I do recommend you do some learning in this area,[32] but here is the quick and dirty on conflict styles. (These are listed in order of least effective to most effective. Read through them and try to recognize yourself in one or two of them.)

Avoiding. This is the style that has you avoiding even the sniff of conflict at all costs. It's a very passive response, and has you tiptoeing around problems, putting everyone else's needs before your own, and agreeing to things you really don't want to agree to. This can be a useful style if you are in a dangerous or abusive situation; but otherwise it's not healthy and it won't be good for you in the long run. Unless you really want a stomach ulcer.

Competing. This style is an aggressive one, in which you have to have the very last word at all costs, and has you being obnoxiously "right" all the time. So there. If you have this conflict style, you are bent on winning every argument, and playing the "I'm better than you" game. It's competitive and argumentative (naturally), and can get

---

[32]See resource section at the end of the book for a list of some of these.

you into serious trouble in the workplace, especially if you happen to be arguing with your supervisor. This is a quick way to be back on the job market search.

Accommodating. This is a passive conflict style that involves putting your own needs, wants, and ideas aside in order to stop the fighting. In this style, you accommodate the other person's needs or wants at the expense of your own. This can serve a purpose in the moment, but can keep you up at night fussing about how mad it makes you that your opinion wasn't considered. There are times when this seems like an easier option, but again, it will come with a cost.

Compromising. This is similar to the accommodating style but is a little less passive. Instead of just giving up your side of the conflict, this style has you bartering a bit to give a little and take a little. In the end, no one is really happy, because no one got exactly what they wanted, and everyone leaves feeling a little used. It's better than some of the styles, but isn't the best choice. Again, it often seems like this is an easier way to work it, and is used a lot in union-versus-management negotiations.

Collaborating. This is an assertive style that is ideal if you can get there. It is what you want to try to work toward having in your conflict resolution skills repertoire. Being collaborative means you are working on the problem to-gether, and coming up with the solution together. Instead of give and take, it treats the problem as the problem (instead of treating the people as the problem), and allows the people to figure out ways to come to a solution.This conflict management style is often the most creative of all of them.

Conflict can happen when we are least expecting it. Sometimes, we don't give enough information to the other person and the result is story-making; the person we've been talking to will leave the conversation with an impression that is inaccurate ... with a story in his or her head about how and why the discussion went the way it did, and this story can be utter fabrication. This is not uncommon. Often, we just assume the other person understands us when perhaps they don't. Because we aren't mind-readers (although, that would be a really useful skill), we are very adept at making up stories to fill in the gaps when not enough information is provided. We then seek other information to support our "made up stories" and if we find it, our stories become our truth. When people are working from two very different stories about what occurred, conflict can and often does ensue.

The goal in effective communication (and in all conversations) is to be as clear as possible, and to provide enough information to the other person to ensure they receive the message you send accurately.

How can you be as clear as possible?

Well, it involves saying more than might feel normal, and giving enough information to be understood correctly. If you are as clear as possible, you leave little room for the story making.

Let me give you some examples.

You are extremely tired from looking after your friend's two-year-old all day the day before, and you really want to go home tonight after work, curl up in your onesie, eat chips, and watch a TV show. There are a couple of your new co-workers who have decided to go to the pub after work, and they invite you along.

You could say, "No, thanks, I can't."

This is not very clear. While it might look clear, it leaves a wide open space for interpretation, or in other words, story making based on perceptions and impressions.

Some possible stories:

- She doesn't like us.
- She doesn't drink.
- She is anti-social.
- She is secretly moonlighting at another job and has to get there in time for her shift.

You really could just keep going here. Some of these made-up stories could cause conflict later on, especially if they are fed with more evidence. (People look for evidence that supports their perceptions and stories. We all do this.) You might have no idea at all that your four-word sentence had such an effect, but that's the problem with conflict: it's complex. The thing is, we have conversations all day long, so why not make them less cryptic, more comprehensive, and less likely to be misunderstood?

If you wanted to stop the story making and be extremely clear about your response, try something like the following and notice the use of "I" language.

You say, "I would really like that, but I'm completely wiped today. I think I overdid it this weekend. I want to just cosy up at home tonight and rest a bit, and I hope you'll invite me another time."

So instead of being cryptic and distant, and just saying, "No thanks," you have given them the real story so they don't have to make one up. They don't have to wonder why you don't want to take them up on their invitation. They now know what you want to do with your evening, and that you would love them to ask you again. This is a friendly, honest, complete, and unapologetic answer, and one that would get you some respect. This response would not be taken personally, and could open up opportunity for the others to be more honest with each other.

HOW TO REDUCE CONFLICT

Identify the problem, first of all. Often people are fighting over two different things and don't even realize it! It is not good enough to imagine you know what the problem is, because then you would be doing that from only your own perspective. Instead, each party needs to name what it is that is bugging them for themselves.

Communicate clearly. Be aware of how you say things, and how they land once you say them, and check in to make sure that what you said made sense to the other person and is working for them. If you catch any discomfort with what's happening, if you sense someone acting upset with you or if you can catch any potential miscommunication at the source, you can often prevent conflict from ever developing, which is ideal. The more developed your communication skills, the less conflict you'll have in your life … and that's my whole aim with Communication Diva.

Use "I" language when you share what's been going on

for you. Again, sharing from your own experience can help someone else see why you're upset. It is never a guarantee, but whatever happens, you can be satisfied in knowing that you weren't accusing or blaming, just telling your side of the story.

Make use of the "pinch-crunch" model. Developed in the 1970s by Jack Sherwood and John Glidewell,[33] it basically works like this (my own interpretation).

Sometimes, when we are in a relationship with someone that is either personal or work-related, things will get said, or something will be done or not done that annoys us. If it's not a big thing, we will feel it as a bit of a "pinch." It annoys us, but it's not bothering us enough to actually do or say anything about it, so we let it go.

Then comes another thing. On its own, it's just small, nothing to get your "knickers in a knot" over, as my grandmother would say, but another pinch. We don't say anything and we let it go, again. After a while though, these pinches add up. We keep ignoring or letting go of the things that bother us, but we don't really let them go either. We stockpile them. We store them up in a box inside us, counting them ... itemizing them ... keeping tabs.

Then one day, the box is full. One more pinch happens and the pressure inside the box is just too much to keep it contained, and we blow up. The little pinches have become one big gigantic crunch and the final pinch, that maybe wasn't really any worse than any of the other little pinches on its own, fuels a huge fight or conflict that at first glance seems irrational and over the top.

---

[33]"Planned Renegotiation: The Pinch Model" The Pfeiffer Library Volume 26, 2nd Edition. Copyright © 1998 Jossey-Bass/Pfeiffer, korcos.wikispaces.com/file/view/Pinch+Crunch.pdf

This is a very dangerous state get into.

And you don't have to.

The best method of conflict resolution is one that is so ancient, it's even found in the Bible! It involves **going directly to the person** you have a "pinch" with, and talking to them about it privately. What this means is not letting your pinch fester and simmer and turn into something bigger than it actually is. Festering and simmering on something that makes you angry simply feeds it and makes it grow. If you deal with it as soon as you possibly can and directly with the person who caused you the pinch, then chances are you can resolve the problem, and truly let it go. This is healthy and will allow you to never build up a box full of pinches that turns into a crunch and is at great risk to escalate into something damaging.

SELF-AWARENESS

Much of what this book is about is developing the skill of self-awareness, in order that you know what you need to work on to improve. It takes a lifetime to know yourself well, and because we humans continue to grow and change and learn with the experiences we gain as we age, the person you thought you knew at age nineteen is going to be significantly different at age forty.

Part of understanding where you can improve involves being able to name your strengths and your limitations. You likely had to answer that question in your interview, and will have to do so again, repeatedly, with each employee performance review.

So, what are your strengths and abilities? Most people find this question very challenging to answer, and yet, taking care in being honest and somewhat humble in the response would be wise.

The next one might not be quite as challenging: Where are your "growing edges"? In other words, where are your weaknesses or limitations?

Everybody has limitations. Yes. Even you do.

It is a really good idea to know the answers to both of these questions, and to be able to articulate them verbally and in writing. You will come across as far more professional to the person doing your employee review if you can clearly state what you need to be working on next, and what you feel you've succeeded in.

When answering these questions, honesty is key, and particularly when naming your limitations. Saying something like, "I'm too organized," is not acceptable. In fact, it sounds arrogant and self-serving. Some "limitations or weaknesses" I've seen listed on resumes are not limitations at all:

"I care about others too much."

"I'm too good of a listener."

Couching a positive attribute in such a way that you call it a weakness is dishonest and raises a red flag, because it indicates to me that the person either doesn't understand the question, or worse, won't admit to having any areas that need improvement.

You will earn respect if you can name a few areas where you would like to improve. I would caution you against giving the reviewer a laundry list of faults, though, as that is damaging and unhelpful to your career advancement. There is no need to invent an answer. People who conduct performance reviews are experienced people. They have seen it all, heard it all, and really want to hear honest and from-the-heart answers.

If you can name two or three areas that you know you could improve in or need to gain experience in, you will show the employer that, firstly, you are actually willing to improve, and secondly, that you are self-aware.

Self-awareness is a prized quality in an employee because it means you will work within your abilities, and won't take on tasks you know you aren't ready to handle or don't understand. In the end, your self-awareness can potentially save the company a lot of trouble and even expense, because you will be less likely to make a major mistake, and less likely to end up burnt out.

It is far better to recognize that you need more experience or training in an area than it is to take it on and then to perform badly.

People (including you) could get hurt.

You could also get unemployed.

If you are having trouble determining where your "growing edges" are, then ask a friend, a parent, a co-worker, or someone you would trust to help you. You need to have a clear and actionable answer for this question, and you need to be sure you make progress on what it is you *say* you need to improve on, so that you can provide a new answer at your next performance review.

Assertiveness: How to Ask for What You Need (*And It's Okay to Say No.*)

Being assertive means respecting yourself just as much

as you are showing respect for the other. It's a very useful way to interact, especially in a workplace setting. It's useful in any setting, really. Those who are aggressive in their behaviour actually lack self-respect as much as they lack respect for others, even though it may be hard to see.

In truth, we all want to be respected. All people, deep down, want to be respected, even the ones who are causing hurt by being aggressive or abusive.

Being passive is also not the answer, and those who do not stand up for themselves for whatever reason, also lack self-respect and the respect of others for them. In a passive behavioural mode, the passive or non-assertive person might be respectful of the person they are interacting with, but in the meantime, they are not honouring their own needs and wishes. This behaviour leads to all sorts of self-esteem and anger issues. People who allow themselves to be crushed—either by a co-worker, a client, or an employer—appear to be unprofessional, as well. Being non-assertive is just as damaging to a career as is being aggressive, and so the ideal is to learn to be assertive.

Being assertive doesn't mean you'll get your own way all the time, nor will it fix all problems, but it does mean the chances of getting what you want at least some of the time will greatly improve.

A Word About Workplace Bullying

Sadly, bullies are not limited to the schoolyard. They grow up into adults who still use the same tactics they have used for dozens of years. I heard about a website that two local counsellors had started to help with workplace bullying, and that they ended up having to shut down because they had day jobs and couldn't keep up with the overwhelming traffic to their site. Learning to be assertive is not going to fix everything, and there are bullies who will make life miserable no matter what you do, but being assertive can definitely help you to navigate the people who would otherwise take advantage of your passive ways.

In an abusive relationship, the person doing the abusing doesn't respect the other person as a human being at all, and the relationship is more about power and control than it is about communicating and working together on a relationship.

The same goes to a lesser extent with an aggressive person, and sometimes the lines between aggression and abuse are blurry.

If you find yourself being bullied in the workplace, there are places to turn to for help. Many employers have employee assistance programs that encourage and cover the costs of an employee speaking confidentially with a counsellor. Many companies have policies and procedures in place for workplace harassment, sexual abuse policies, and complaint procedures. Reading those policies and procedures can guide you as to how to proceed if you need help. It might be that you can seek the advice and help of a manager or supervisor. In situations where there are no policies in place, you may need to look outside the organization to the Human Rights Commission. The sad thing about workplace bullying, besides how widespread it is, is that it takes a certain amount of assertiveness and courage to address it effectively, and often those being bullied feel alone, afraid, and unable to take the steps needed.

The main benefit of being assertive and of having assertiveness as your default behaviour is that you will be seen as professional. You will be less prone to being taken advantage of; you will be able to tell others what it is you need and want; you will be respectful of others even in disagreements; and you will be earning the respect of others.

SO, WHAT DOES BEING AN ASSERTIVE PERSON LOOK LIKE?

You Stand Up for Yourself.

Assertive people don't allow others to say or do things that are unfair to them, without saying something about it. Standing up for yourself in a calm, but firm way is a sign of assertiveness. Naming very clearly how the words or behaviour of the other person have affected you—how you feel about it—is an effective skill.[34]

You Make Your Own Choices.

Assertive people have a say in what goes on, and don't let others decide or dictate what happens without having some input. Assertive people make thoughtful decisions while respecting their own needs and the needs of others.

You Act Instead of React.

If you're assertive, you'll act according to your own values and beliefs, and try not to react to the actions of others. This is really (really) hard to do for many of us, and it takes

---

[34]What you say might not make any difference to how things turn out in the end, because you have no control over what other people actually do, but you'll have the satisfaction of knowing you said something in the first place.

a lot of practice, but it means doing what you think, know, and feel to be the right thing, despite what others around you say or do.

You Respect Boundaries.

The assertive person respects the boundaries of others, as well as their own. They don't let others cross lines they shouldn't, and they try to be respectful of the boundaries others have put up. This is very different from how an aggressive person acts. An aggressive person crosses all sorts of boundaries all the time, and doesn't care or even notice that it's happening. A passive (non-assertive) person lets their own boundaries be run over constantly. An assertive person who has clearly stated boundaries gains respect from others a lot faster and more easily, because they aren't afraid to let others know when they are getting close to crossing a line.

You Are Comfortable With Yourself.

An assertive person is comfortable in their own skin. (This doesn't mean they don't want to look good, or anything; it just means they are not always trying to impress). This person doesn't feel the need to put others down in order to feel good. This person doesn't feel the need to build themselves up by bragging or boasting in order to feel worthy. This person has a healthy respect for him or herself, and a good knowledge of what limitations and weaknesses he or she needs to work on.

SOME OF THE BENEFITS OF BEING ASSERTIVE

So why would this skill be useful or helpful or desirable to have in the workplace? Well, lots of reasons, and here are some of them.

Assertion Prevents Stress.

People who are aggressive stress other people out. People who are passive often experience stress as a result of the unhappiness and anger that builds up inside because of all the lack of respect and hurt they are taking in.

Saying what you need and what you want, in an assertive way, alleviates stress and can help you to be a healthier person. And who doesn't want to be healthier? This happens whether you actually get what you need or want or not.

Assertion Can Prevent Confrontation.

Sometimes, clear, assertive communication can prevent the build-up of stress and anger that can lead to a major blow-up. If someone does something that upsets you, annoys you, or makes you mad, telling them how you feel immediately will get it out of your system and prevent you from letting it fester. Festering resentment can build and grow and then blow up, a common thing that happens to passive people. Dealing with things that bother you as they arise is much healthier, as mentioned earlier in the "Pinch-Crunch" theory discussion.

Assertive People Earn Respect.

I know I've said this a few times now, but it bears repeating: you will find that the more you can be assertive, especially in a professional setting, the more respect you will earn from others.

Assertive people set boundaries, make decisions, don't treat others or themselves badly, are collaborative, and are generally easier to work with.

Assertive people don't play games.

Being assertive can reduce miscommunication and prevent mistakes.

Assertive people are often better communicators.

Assertiveness allows a person to say what they *really* want to say, instead of saying what they think the other person wants to hear. It is quite possible to say something like, "I don't agree with you, but I'll go along with the decision so that we can move forward and let the record show I am not in agreement." That is an assertive statement, even though the outcome is not what the other person would like to see happen. It's crystal clear communication.

So what happens if you need to get more assertive?

Well, you can practise! Practise in situations that don't matter as much as your workplace does. For example, be assertive (not abusive or mean) to telephone solicitors who interrupt you at dinnertime. Be firm and clear with salespeople in the stores. When you have mastered behaving this way with strangers, test it out on friends or family members who ask or expect you to do things you don't want to do. See what happens. Assertive *skills* are called skills because they take time and practice.

Here's a list of skills that can be worked on to help you

develop your assertiveness muscle, and, like any other type of skill, this won't happen overnight. Start with small things and work your way into bigger things that have a bigger result or consequence. The trick is to actually *start!*

PRACTISE SAYING NO.

One thing assertive people do is say no when they need to. This is a skill that can be practised ... and it's easy to practise, especially if you are someone who gets those awful dinnertime telephone solicitation calls, where a salesperson is trying desperately to talk you into buying some product or service. You can use the "broken-record" technique. This involves calmly and clearly repeating your position, sometimes multiple times, without getting hooked emotionally by whatever the other person is saying.

The example I use most often is the one where the kids at my house want dessert but don't want to finish their dinners. I say over and over (like a broken record or a skipping cd for you modern-folk) "You can have dessert when you have finished your dinner." Eventually, they stop talking when they figure out that my position is not going to change no matter what hysterics, rationalizations, bargaining, or pleading is going on. The same technique works with the dinner solicitation calls. When the salesperson finishes his or her pitch, I am polite, calm, and repetitive. I say something like, "We aren't interested in a lawn care package at this time, thank you." I may need to say it three or four times, until eventually the person hears my message. I'm firm, clear, and never rude when I do this, because after all, the person calling is just doing his or her job.

You can try this technique when you run up against peer pressure, high-pressure sales in stores, and all sorts of other situations where you want to say no. It really works, but the trick is to keep strong in your position and not back down.

PRACTISE DECISIVENESS

If you are passive, you might find that it's hard for you to give a clear answer when asked a question. Instead of being honest, you start to worry about what the other person is going to think of you, and you want to please them, so you tell them what you think it is *they* want to hear. Or you don't really give any answer, and in effect completely avoid making any kind of decision.

Sound familiar?

This allows you, as a passive person, to complain later about what happened, because of course, it wasn't you who suggested whatever it is that happened.

So, instead, the ultimate goal is to actually say what it is you really want. (There is naturally no guarantee you'll get it, but at least you can feel inside that you contributed.)

Start practising with simple things, like answering truthfully the question: "What should we have for dinner?" Or when out at a restaurant and you have to choose some food, practise doing that a little faster than usual, and don't pay too much attention to what anyone else is ordering. Order what you want to eat. Practise naming what you want, and do it without worrying about what might make other people happy. If you can make your own decisions, beginning with little things like what song you want played next, or what movie to go see, you'll become more comfortable with bigger decisions.

Practise Socializing

Social settings can be intimidating for shy and passive people. If you're working in a job that requires human interaction (for example, in the medical field, in a service industry, in any job where you need to talk to others in order to get your work done) and you are shy and quiet, you might not be working as efficiently as you could be. People come in every kind of package, and some are easier to work with and get along with than others. If being around people is a painful and challenging experience for you, it could just be that you need to build up your skill set a little.

Being able to walk into a room full of people and strike up a conversation with a random stranger might not sound like your idea of a fun time, but it's a brilliant way to start flexing your skill-building muscles, and to get more comfortable with figuring out how to relate to people. You can try this by speaking to strangers in the line-up at the grocery store, at the bus stop, or anywhere in public that you find yourself. It might seem scary and hard at first, but I promise you, you won't die, and after a while, it will get easier.

Of course, sometimes, assertiveness is not going to get you what you need or want with regards to your employer, especially if you are in a situation where you will be "punished" for standing up for yourself. Use caution and proceed with baby steps.

Remember, you have a few choices:

1. You can let people take advantage of you and make

decisions for you (which will definitely *not* improve your professionalism), and you can continue to be unhappy.

2. You can respect yourself and others by setting clear boundaries around what you will or will not (or can or cannot) do.

3. You can leave the situation. You may not be able to truly do that with your sister, but you can leave an employment situation. What happens after you do, however, may be interesting, depending upon what you have for viable options. It may not be the best choice, but in the end, it is still a choice. Staying in a job situation where you are not respected can make you physically ill. It might be better in the end to rethink this and make some changes.

Before We Finish

In Conclusion

And so, here we are, almost at the end of this book. If you did pick it up at a garage sale,[35] I hope it was worth ten times what you paid for it!

If someone gave it to you as a gift, I hope you thank them profusely for their choice.

If you are reading this as part of a class, then thank your teacher for being so wise in adding it to the curriculum.

All kidding aside, I said at the start that my hope and my goal are that after going through this book, you are able to come across to others as truly professional, and as an outstanding choice in an employee.

I also expect that even if you don't have the job you want yet, you have a better understanding of what it takes to be not just a good employee, but to be an **excellent** one, in whatever kind of work you take on.

My even bigger dream is that you will have grown as a person along the way too, and that you will trust yourself a little more, believe in yourself and your capabilities, and not be afraid to just go for it ... whatever "it" happens to be.[36]

Here is one last story for you.

---

[35]Heaven forbid!
[36]Unless we're talking about getting a date with the girl in switchboard. I can't help you with that one.

The Hotdog Man

There is a man in my town who has a hotdog stand outside the local big box grocery store. He is a bit of a local icon. Yes, he sells hotdogs and bags of chips and cans of pop, and he does that part of it just fine ... but Miguel is so much more than a guy selling you lunch. Miguel is one of the hardest-working people I know. He's there first thing in the morning and all day long, and doesn't ever seem to take a day off. Miguel always has time to talk, reads books between chats and serving customers, has a psychology degree, and knows a lot about music. And Miguel is more than that too.

Miguel *gets* people.

He interacts with hundreds of people a day. For some it's a whole conversation, for others, it's just a friendly hello, and others it can even just be a smile, but it's the fact that he goes over and above the mere selling of hotdogs. He is not a salesman. He is, as Seth Godin would say, an artist.

Miguel's recall of names is something else, and his ability to be genuine and real and to connect with people is truly a gift. Miguel is someone you look forward to smiling and waving at from the parking lot, because you just know that if he sees you, he'll be someone who lights up your day with his huge "Hello!" that makes you feel like you are the most important person in the universe in that moment.

And I'm not the only one who feels this way. I happen to know a group of twenty-year-old boys who, as teenagers, would go to the store just to see Miguel and buy hotdogs and have a chat with him. Of course, he remembered all their names. I even know people who have gone to the hotdog stand for dinner, between after-school basketball and evening soccer practice. My husband jokes about being a big spender and taking his family "out to Miguel's" for dinner when we are busy going "hither and yon."[37] The fact that almost everyone in this town knows his name is testament to his ability to be so generous with himself ... and that's what it's about. As I said before, he *gets* it. He might not be a high-powered CEO of a multimillion-dollar company. He doesn't even have an office or a desk. In fact, he doesn't even have four walls and it gets mighty cold in the winter in his tin shed. He makes his living in a way that many of us wouldn't want to and couldn't even imagine doing. He's a hotdog salesman ... but it isn't even about the food. For Miguel, it's all about relationship.

Back in 2009, the grocery chain made the decision to close down their hotdog stands. There was such a huge outcry from this community when they heard that Miguel might have to close up shop, that a Facebook page was formed, hundreds of letters of pleading and outrage were written to the owner, and a petition with more than five thousand names was signed. In the end (and to the company's credit, which is partly why I still shop at that store) Miguel's hotdog stand was allowed to stay, and is still there.

---

[37] I have always wanted to use that phrase! Try dropping it into your next conversation just for fun and see what happens.

I can't eat gluten, so I don't actually buy the hotdogs anymore, but I still look forward to his loud, "Hello, Jenn!" whenever I go by his stand to go into the store, and if he's not surrounded by numerous other people (which often, he is), I'll stop for a chat ... because he is who he is and he's making a difference by being who he is with authenticity, generosity, and compassion.

Miguel is a person who sparks something good in other people just by being truly himself, and by offering that to others.

This book isn't about changing who you are as a human being. You are unique and gifted, and have something to offer the world by being just who YOU are.

What I hope you've come to understand by now is that you'll be able to be that wonderful you at work: only maybe now you will be a "you" who has developed a few good habits and practices along the way; a "you" who is more self-aware and able to pay attention to your own presence in the world; a "you" who is authentic and generous, humble and compassionate to those around you; a "you" who is the absolute best, most professional "you" you can be.

This is my hope for you.

Most of us have to work our entire lives just to be able to pay the bills and to have the things and experiences we would like to have. Putting some effort into how you show up (in every sense of that word) in your job, can make the difference between just working to earn a paycheque (how sad) and actually getting some pleasure and satisfaction out of the work that you do.

If you have to work anyway, why not use it as an opportunity to learn about the work you are doing, to learn about yourself, and to learn how to excel in what you are doing?

May all good things come your way.
May you live with great compassion and with real
generosity.
May you pass this brilliant and useful book onto to
someone you love ...
and may you be the most professional person you
can be as you stand out and shine in your new job.
Peace,
Jennifer

Bonus

The Thirty-Day Risk Challenge

This bonus section is included to help you take the next step in standing out and shining both at work and in other areas of your life. It is an idea that was introduced to me by a friend, and one that I wanted to share with you, the reader. It is based on the idea that one of the best ways to challenge yourself to grow as a person, to create new opportunities for yourself, and to get more assertive and less shy, is to take risks.

I don't necessarily mean bungee jumping or sky diving, although those would definitely be classified as risky; I mean small things that might not be scary for other people, but that move you out of your own "comfort zone."

Doing this can do all sorts of things for you. It can:

- increase your self-confidence
- help you meet new and interesting people
- expand your knowledge so you can have better conversations with others
- help you to meet goals
- motivate you
- inspire you
- be fun!

What would you consider to be something that might push you a little?

I got the idea of taking risks every day for a month as a challenge from a friend and business consultant named Lynn Oucharek of O Vision Consulting.[38] Lynn created a challenge for her clients and followed it herself and then blogged about it, and she has allowed me to share the idea with you. This is my version of it.

Here are four areas you might want to consider looking at:

1. NOT THE SAME OLD, SAME OLD.

If you always do the same old thing and look at the same things online, then you aren't expanding your horizons. You can very easily (and with zero expense) spend some time doing some research into areas that you never normally would. Check out something you have never looked at before on Pinterest. Go to websites that have nothing to do with anything you are interested in or that you know nothing about, and spend some time learning. You never know what ideas might come out of this time, what inspiration you will find, what new people you will discover.

Do you know anything about scuba diving? Have you thought about photography? What about musical theatre, or raw food recipes, upright gardening, greyhound dogs, 3D printing, motor cycles, architecture, wet shaving (which is apparently making a come-back), or how shoe laces are made? I recently watched a short video on how Lego is made and the history of Lego, and it was really cool and made me want to go find some and build something.

[38]www.ovisionconsulting.com

How is this risky, you might ask? Well, it isn't scary risky ... it's just outside what you might normally ever do or look at, and that's a baby step in the right direction, from the safety of your own home. It's good to challenge yourself.

One way to find ideas is to listen to conversations you have with others or that you hear other people having in coffee shops or lineups. Make note of the topic and go home and learn a little about it. You never know what might come of it; it will give you a bit of knowledge if you find yourself talking to someone who is into that particular thing (which could very well impress him or her, by the way), and you just don't know what could happen next.

One of my all-time favourite sayings is: "You just never know what'll happen in a day."

And you don't. So go explore and expand yourself!

2. It's All About the Details.

We do things, and sometimes we do things by rote ... automatically and without even thinking about it.

Have you ever gone somewhere and wondered when you got there, *how* you actually got there?

When we do that, when we don't pay attention and are not really present to what's going on, we miss things.

We miss opportunities.

When you travel, you notice a lot more because you are out of your normal circumstances and you aren't used to things you are seeing, tasting, and feeling. Even the air seems different, and you might notice it, whereas at home, you wouldn't.

We were on vacation in the Caribbean a couple of years ago and were absolutely delighted to see these huge iguanas near a tennis court when we were out for a walk. We went over close to them and took pictures and checked out how colourful they were and how weird they actually look. It was pretty exciting ... at first.

After a week of being there and seeing iguanas everywhere, it was no longer very interesting. The locals were probably rolling their eyes at us ... the same way we do here in North America when we see tourists taking pictures of squirrels.

But when we don't notice the details and the everyday normal things we take for granted, we miss a lot..

Lynn suggests taking a couple of items out of your household gadget drawer.[39] Make sure these are two things that don't naturally go together. Make a game with them, with rules and everything, and invite friends or family to play your new game. Then ask them for feedback on the game.

The idea is that next time you are out somewhere doing something ordinary, take a look around you. Pay attention to things you normally wouldn't (like a two-year-old would, or a puppy, for that matter) and see what you can do with it.

What new and interesting ideas can you come up with? If you were a tourist, what do you think you would notice on your walk or drive home that you haven't noticed before?

A dad I know got some stickers that look like big googly eyes. He and his kids spent an afternoon walking around the neighbourhood putting "eyes" on inanimate objects! Suddenly metal fence posts and fire hydrants and all sorts of other everyday items looked alive and funny, and

---

[39]Almost everyone has a gadget drawer, or a box or a bag or a bowl full of things you don't know what to do with. Like bread clips. I dislike bread clips intensely. I have no idea why, but I do.

probably made a lot of other people laugh too when they walked past.

Delight in the details, and you might be surprised what comes of it.

3. GET BUSY.

Make things happen. If you are someone who creates things (music, writing, blog posts, videos, podcasts, pies, lamps, paintings, sweaters, whatever) then make them and put them out there for the world to see. Show your creation to at least one other person and get feedback.

It's okay if it isn't perfect or even any good. You will learn by doing.

You also don't have to create some major masterpiece the first time around. You can just begin with something small, and "test the waters," as it were.

See what happens. Get feedback. Create again.

Waiting until it's perfect or brilliant or so amazing you can't stand it might actually mean you have to wait forever. In other words, you might never even bother ... because the chances of your hitting the "next greatest thing ever" jackpot on your first try are probably as good as winning that lottery. It's easier to just skip buying the ticket in the first place, right?

But then, you'll never actually get anywhere.

I suggest starting small. Make a small goal, write it down, and go do it.

If you want to make new friends or new connections, then make them. Reach out and give it a shot. Call someone you haven't talked to for a long time. Say hello to that quiet neighbour you'd like to know. This doesn't have to be huge ... it can be just the beginning.

And yes, it could be risky. You will feel yourself s-t-r-e-t-c-h, which is what risking or challenging ourselves is all about.

If it goes over well, you will learn something.

If it fails, you will also learn something.

Doing nothing is always easier, and you won't get anywhere fast by doing it ... so doing nothing is not an option if you plan to stand out and shine.

Ideas are just ideas until you put them into action. Chances are, you have several great ideas, and implementing them could be a little scary at first ... but think of what **can't ever happen** unless you at least try.

You really don't want to be one of those people who spends his or her twilight years living in regret because you were too afraid to try something, too afraid to risk a little, or too afraid of what might happen if what you were trying for didn't work.

4. Volunteer Much?

You might have had to volunteer for credit in school. At least, you do here in this part of the world ... and although you might have grumbled about it at the time, I bet you got something out of it in the end.

Volunteering might feel a little more risky, because often you have to put yourself in situations you aren't normally in, you have to talk to strangers, and you have to do things you might not normally do. Volunteering can put you into instant community, which, for some people, can be a little uncomfortable and even a little risky.

All brilliant ways for you to grow as a person.

Giving back to a community you care about or a

community that means something to you is a great way to expand. It could be anything from signing a petition to starting a website, from helping at a local soup kitchen to taking someone to a doctor's appointment, from offering your support to a cause you believe in to participating in a protest march, from walking your elderly neighbour's dog to making a casserole for someone who is sick, from cleaning up trash from your street to visiting someone in hospital, from helping out at a local church or community centre to teaching someone a skill you happen to possess ... the list is endless.

What does giving back do for you?

Well, it can help you grow as a person, that's for sure.

Giving back is about someone *other* than you.

Giving back is sneaky, because while you are doing something for someone or something else ... you actually "get" something in return. You actually gain in the end.

It might be risky, if you have to get off the couch and out into the world in order to do it.

It might push you to stand up for what you truly believe in.

It might test you physically, mentally, or emotionally.

It might ignite something inside you that you didn't know existed.

It might just change the world.

So, choose a new challenge every day for an entire month. Write down what you are going to do, go do it, and report back to someone about what you did and what you learned. This last part will keep you accountable.

If you keep a record of this (journal, blog, Facebook, whatever), then you can go back over your learnings at the end of the thirty days and see what there is to discover about yourself and how you've changed.

If you fail at something along the way, great![40]

If something happens that you weren't expecting, even better.

Challenging yourself in this way pushes boundaries and opens up worlds. If record labels didn't ever risk, we wouldn't know most of the artists we love to listen to. If casting directors didn't take chances on that unknown actor, we wouldn't discover some of the talent that is out there. If inventors didn't keep trying, we wouldn't have automatic coffee machines. If the snack-food makers didn't keep trying, we wouldn't have Oreos. If writers didn't bother, you wouldn't be reading helpful books like this one right about now.

You have so much more to discover about who you are and what you are capable of.

So why wait?

---

[40]See the section on failing being a good thing sometimes. You never know what brilliance might come out of what you try to do.

Resources

The following is a short list of books that I have found to be useful and inspiring, and which you might explore if you want to take your learning about professionalism in the workplace deeper.

Communication

Goleman, Daniel. *Emotional Intelligence: Why It Can Matter More Than IQ.* Toronto, ON: Bantam Books, 1996.

Goleman, Daniel. *Destructive Emotions: A Scientific Dialogue with the Dalai Lama.* New York, NY: Bantam Books, 2003.

Chernoff, Sandy. *5 Secrets to Effective Communication: Creating Meaningful Relationships & Enhanced Happiness in Your Business.* Canada: Soft Skills for Success, 2014

Covey, Stephen R. *The 7 Habits of Highly Effective People: Powerful Lessons in Personal Change.* New York, NY: Simon and Schuster, 2004.

Covey, Stephen R. *The 8th Habit: From Effectiveness to Greatness.* New York, NY: Free Press, 2004.

Conflict

Covey, Stephen R. *The 3rd Alternative: Solving Life's Most Difficult Problems.* New York, NY: Free Press, 2011.

Scott, Susan. *Fierce Conversations: Achieving Success at Work and in Life One Conversation at a Time.* New York, NY: The Berkley Publishing Group, 2002.

Donaldson, Michael C. *Negotiating for Dummies.* Hoboken, NJ: Wiley Publishing Inc., 2007.

Inspiration

I like anything that Seth Godin has written, but here are three of my favourites:

Godin, Seth. *Linchpin: Are You Indispensable?* New York, NY: Portfolio (the Penguin Group), 2010.

Godin, Seth. *Tribes: We Need You to Lead Us.* New York, NY: Portfolio (the Penguin Group), 2008.

Godin, Seth. *What to Do When It's Your Turn: And It's Always Your Turn.* USA: Seth Godin, 2014.

Sinek, Simon. *Start With Why: How Great Leaders Inspire Everyone to Take Action.* New York, NY: Portfolio (the Penguin Group), 2009.

Stress Management

Carlson, Richard. *Don't Sweat the Small Stuff and It's All Small Stuff: Simple Ways to Keep the Little Things From Taking Over Your Life.* New York, NY: Hyperion, 1997.

Jensen, Bill. *The Simplicity Survival Handbook.* New York, NY: Basic Books, 2003.

Time Management

Tracy, Brian. *Eat That Frog!: 21 Great Ways to Stop Procrastinating and Get More Things Done in Less Time.* San Francisco, CA: Berrett-Koehler Publishers, Inc., 2007.

Allen, David. *Getting Things Done: The Art of Stress-Free Productivity.* New York, NY: Penguin Books, 2003.

Duhigg, Charles. *The Power of Habit: Why We Do What We Do in Life and Business.* New York, NY: Random House, 2014.

Author Biography

 Jennifer Swanson has been teaching Communication and Human Relation skills since 1993 to college students entering the medical field. She is also the creator/host of the Communication Diva Podcast, which has an international audience and helps people in deepening workplace and personal relationships through more effective communication. In addition to teaching young adults, Swanson is an ordained minister in the United Church of Canada, has worked in the Youth and Family Ministry for three years, has a Master's Degree in Public and Pastoral Leadership, and is a certified conflict coach and Master NLP Practitioner. She is also a mother and step-mother to two young adults and two teens. Swanson draws upon years of expertise as she shares her passion for inspiring others to reach their full potential with readers and audiences worldwide.

Jennifer Swanson shares her passion for clear communication and offers skills training, insights and hands-on learning experiences as a workshop leader, speaker, and podcast host, at conferences, employee education days, in churches, schools, and in other group settings.

As a speaker, she includes engaging stories, examples and insights from her more than two decades of working and teaching in the healthcare field.

Jennifer's dream is to help inspire others to grow into their full potential, and to help the world be a more gentle place through deeper and more life-giving relationships.

To learn more please visit:
www.communicationdiva.com

To contact Jennifer Swanson:
jenn@communicationdiva.com

Twitter:
@JennSwanson2

If you want to get on the path to becoming a published author with Influence Publishing please go to www.InfluencePublishing.com

Inspiring books that influence change

More information on our other titles and how to submit your own proposal can be found at www.InfluencePublishing.com